MUDPIES TO MAGNETS

MUDPIES
TO
MAGNETS

A Preschool Science Curriculum

Robert A. Williams
Robert E. Rockwell
Elizabeth A. Sherwood

Illustrations by
Laurel J. Sweetman

Gryphon House, Inc.
Mt. Rainier, Maryland

*We dedicate this book
to the Children,
Parents,
and Teachers
who responded
so warmly to
Hug A Tree—*

FOREWORD

Jessica and Michael are working hard at the work bench. The body of their car has been carefully chosen and the wheels have been nailed on with vigor. Now comes the test drive. "Teacher our wheels won't go!"

Alicia has just completed a painting. Mr. Casey has told her that when it is dry, she may take it home to show her family. Her response is, "Where does the wet go when it dries?"

Out on the playground the climber is being attacked by aliens. The space heros respond with blasts from their laser guns. One morning, there are several new books on a table in the classroom. They contain all sorts of pictures of astronauts, spacecraft and other exciting things. On the wall is a poster of an astronaut on the moon and below it sits a model of the space shuttle.

Events such as these are a vital part of teaching science. As adults involved with children, we can capitalize on everyday experiences by adding to them other, carefully planned activities. By doing so, we let children know that curiosity can lead to learning and that what they want to know is important. Viewed in this manner, science, defined as knowledge gained through observations, study, and experimentation, is what life is about for children, even the very young.

The children bring with them a body of knowledge and experiences. Our role is to find out what they know and work from there. The advantage of the child-directed approach to teaching is that it allows the children to work at levels appropriate to their skills, interest, and needs. Children can begin at different levels and yet be involved in the entire instructional process. However, spontaneous experiences alone cannot be relied on to provide a well-balanced science curriculum. There must be planning to create a program which covers a wide range of topics, includes the repetition needed for mastery, and occurs in a sequence which allows for growth and development.

In planning, it must be remembered that acquisition of facts is not the goal of science for young children. Instead, we want the children to experience the success and joy that come from finding the answers to questions by doing things rather than by being told. In many simple ways, they can repeatedly be thrilled by their discoveries, particularly if the adults around them share their enthusiasm. Adult reaction, both verbal and nonverbal, to the activities of children has a major impact. If children sense disappointment or another negative response, uninhibited exploring will soon be replaced by that classic school phenomenon, looking for the "right" answer. If, instead, a teacher can convey a sense of wonder and delight in our world, children will soon respond in the same way. In fact, they may look at something in a way that is novel and fresh and not at all what you had in mind. You may end up being the learner.

Because we feel that an integrated approach to teaching science is best, we have divided the activity section of the book into chapters based on areas commonly used in classroom arrangement and curriculum planning. Also, it is important to have an area in the classroom set aside especially for science materials and activities. Information about how to develop such an area is included in the THINGS YOU WILL NEED section. Just as important, is working toward making science an integral part of your day and a meaningful experience for the children. The section entitled, WHAT TO DO, will assist you in planning these experiences.

Mudpies to Magnets can also be helpful in developing the interests of individual children. Activities related to the subject of their interest, whether it be a flashlight, a rock, a magnet, or a feather, can be found through the index and explored in as much detail as time and enthusiasm allow. This sort of spontaneous learning does much to encourage a curious and questioning attitude in children. They are much more likely to continue to explore objects and ideas if they are supported in their endeavors by a thoughtful and curious adult.

Explorations in science help children gradually make the transition from the world of magic and the unpredictable, to the adult world of facts, information, and the delights of real discovery. Children are developing skills in thinking, reasoning, and observing which will be of value in all areas of their lives. It was Robert Frost who said "Sunset is always in horizontal layers. This is science, but it is poetry, too." Encourage an appreciation for both the science and poetry the children find. The experience will delight everyone.

The age appropriateness given for each activity is an approximate, and is based upon our observations of many children who have tried them. Remember, each child has a particular backlog of experience which will guide any responses to an activity. The children and their reactions should be the final judges of whether the activity is appropriate for them or not.

CONTENTS

FOREWORD vii
WORDS YOU CAN USE: Talking With Children About Science 11
THINGS YOU WILL NEED: Setting Up for Science 13
SCIENCE SAFETY: Build Good Habits Early 14
RESOURCES 15
FINDING THE THINGS YOU WILL NEED 16
WHAT TO DO: Some Thoughts on Teaching Science 18
YOUNG CHILDREN AND LEARNING 20
SOME IDEAS ABOUT PLANNING 21
WANT TO DO MORE: Making Your Own Science Kits 24

ON YOUR OWN:
SCIENCE CENTER ACTIVITIES

2+ Minimuseums 27
2+ Pill Bug Palace 28
2+ The Great Air Machine Race 29
2+ The Main Attraction: Magnet
　　　Boxes 30
3+ Dancing Droppers 31
3+ Fish—Up Close and Personal 32
3+ Oh I Seed You 33
3+ Shadow Box 34
3+ Shake, Shake, Shake 35
3+ Touchy Feely Box 36
4+ Big Dipper, Little Dipper, Everyone's
　　　a Star 37
4+ Cling to Me 38
4+ Put a Rock to Bed 39
4+ Put Them in a Row 40
4+ Real Puzzles 41
4+ Seed Power 42
4+ Texture Collage: Take Your Fingers
　　　for a Walk 43
5+ Sound Traveler 44

BUILDING WITH SCIENCE:
CONSTRUCTION AND MEASUREMENT

2+ Balancing Toys 47
2+ Pulley into Line 48
3+ Can I Make a Shape? 49

3+ Newspaper Construction 50
3+ Rampin' It 51
4+ Call Me 52
4+ Rolling, Rolling, Rolling 53
5+ Cave in a Box 54
5+ Dinosaur Den 55
5+ Turning Mud Pies into Houses . . . 56
5+ Where Do You Hide a
　　　Dinosaur? 57

SCIENCE FOR A CROWD:
CIRCLE TIME ACTIVITIES

2+ Rainbow in a Jar 61
3+ Bags of Energy 62
3+ Thunk or Ding 63
3+ What's That Sound? 64
4+ Lightning & Thunder, Wow It's
　　　Scary 64
4+ Mushy, Slushy, Melty Snow 66
4+ Ticket to the Moon 67
4+ Weather or Not I Should Wear it . . 68
4+ What's the Color of the Day 69
4+ Zero and Counting 70
5+ Dino Tongue Twister 71
5+ I've Got a Hunch, Seed 72
5+ Let There Be Light 73
5+ Shadow, Shadow on the Wall 74

PAINTS AND PRINTS:
SCIENTIFIC ART

2+	Color My Petals	77
2+	Eye Dropper Art	78
2+	Rainbow Rain	79
2+	Rainbow Stew	79
3+	Beat a Leaf	80
3+	Paper Chromatography	81
3+	Weather Art	82
3+	Weaving Nature's Colors	83
3+	Put the Sunny Side Up	84
4+	Beans in a Jar	85
4+	Fingerprints: No Two Alike	86
4+	Magical Magnet Masterpieces	87
4+	Rough and Smooth	88

WET AND MESSY:
SCIENCE FOR A SPECIAL PLACE

2+	Magic Matter	91
2+	The Dunking Raisins	92
3+	Drying Race	93
3+	Egg Carton Rainbows	94
3+	Floaters and Sinkers	95
3+	I'm Forever Blowing Bubbles	96
3+	Let's Get Soaked	97
3+	Pendulum Patterns in the Sand	98
3+	Shine Your Pennies	99
4+	Grow a Rock	100
4+	Thermometer Play	101
4+	Soak It to Me	102
5+	Fill It Up: A Question of Volume	103
5+	Raincycle	104

SCIENCE TO GROW ON:
HEALTH AND NUTRITION

3+	Body Game	107
3+	Good and Juicy	108
3+	Little Bitty Butter Beaters	109
3+	Orange You Glad They're Not All Alike?	110
3+	Ouchie	111
3+	Sprouts	112
4+	Keep It Cool	113
4+	Listen to the Sounds of the Body	114
4+	My, How You Have Grown!	115
4+	Sing Along	116
5+	Bones Builders: Skeleton Creators	117
5+	Robots Have Bodies Too	118
5+	Snack Graphing	119
5+	The Great Brush Off	120

LEARNING ABOUT NATURE:
OUTDOOR SCIENCE

3+	Ant E Social	123
3+	Collect a Mural	124
3+	Shirts in the Sun	125
3+	Teeny, Tiny Tweezer Trek	126
3+	Twig Race	127
4+	How Many Colors Are Green?	128
4+	Leaf Catchers	129
4+	Outdoor Hunt and Find	131
4+	Puddle Walk	133
4+	Your Own Animal Book	134
5+	Rain Measures	135
5+	Warble, Cheep or Tweet: Name That Tune	136

ACTING OUT SCIENCE IN A BIG WAY:
CREATIVITY AND MOVEMENT

3+	Dance a Garden	139
3+	Dino Body Match!	140
3+	Leaf Hunt Relay	141
3+	Sensitive Toes	142
3+	Space Helmets	143
4+	Color Makers	144
4+	Marching of the Seasons	145
4+	Stepping Out, Hop, Skip, Jump	146
4+	The Purr-fect Smell	147
4+	Weather Predictors	148
5+	Flashlight Tag	149
5+	The Shape and Hop Game	150

HODGE-PODGE

Tornado in a Jar	151
Ocean in a Jar	152
Critter Cage	152
Hanger Sorter	153
The Best Resource Sources	154

WORDS YOU CAN USE: TALKING WITH CHILDREN ABOUT SCIENCE

*T*alking with children about their activities, whether in science or another area, can clarify or confirm their understanding. An important part of this is asking questions. Thought provoking questions, whether they come from you or the children, can do much to expand an ordinary experience. If the children are in the midst of an activity and simply want information, a straightforward answer is the best response. At other times, helping them arrive at the answer themselves may be most satisfying. You can direct them to resources, either people or books, ask questions which may head them in a new direction, or suggest some materials or ideas which might help.

Now and then you will have children who don't ask many questions. In that case, ask some yourself. Comments such as, "I wonder where those ants are going?" may be enough to start a child thinking. Be sure that you are there to help look for the answer or at least start them in the right direction. Random "thinking" questions such as "Will more water or Jell-O fit in a spoon?" or "How can you know the wind is blowing when you're inside?" Can be used during odd moments of the day. They improve both reasoning skills and language usage.

If independent thinking is what we want to develop, in the children, we adults must learn to wait for it. Try waiting for a short time after asking a question. The quality as well as the quantity of answers will improve noticeably. Discuss both accurate and inaccurate answers with children. This allows children to see that all answers are worth some thought. You'll also discover that many times children with right answers know little more than those with wrong ones. This was clearly demonstrated by a child who could say with confidence, "The water evaporated." Upon further questioning it became apparent that the child had no idea of what evaporation meant, but was simply repeating what she had been told. It is wise to remember that words are only labels for concepts. Just because children can repeat the labels does not mean that they understand the concepts. Investigating the children's responses will give you a better idea of their knowledge and experiences and enable you to plan additional activities effectively.

Children need to be given accurate information. The quantity given will vary with individual needs, but what is shared should be correct. It's better to say "I don't know" than to foster misconceptions. Your lack of information can be used to show children the value of using resources. The visual memory and attention to detail required to find a bird in a guide book is invaluable for cognitive development. Children must organize their thoughts if they want to ask questions of the custodian to find out what happens to water when it goes down the drain. Books take on new meaning when it is discovered that they have pictures which show how to make a doorbell that really buzzes.

Encourage speculation by being accepting of the children's responses. For example:

Where do you suppose clouds get the water to make rain?

Probably smoke.

Why smoke?

Didn't you ever see smoke before? (obviously they look alike, therefore . . .)

Remember that complex, creative thinking and problem solving takes practice. Give them time to learn. After talking awhile, it is often useful to close such a discussion with some kind of summary. For example: "Some people think clouds get water from smoke, some think from swimming pools, some think the old rain goes back to the sky." Such a conversation can lead to further exploration if it seems useful and interesting. It might be the right time to introduce an activity on the water cycle! As a final note, remember that the children with limited verbal abilities will often surprise you with their skills if they are allowed to demonstrate rather than tell about a subject. You can then use this knowledge to help promote their language development by working with the strengths they have.

THINGS YOU WILL NEED: SETTING UP FOR SCIENCE

Although this book is designed to teach science in every part of the classroom, attention should be given to the heart of the science program, the Science Center. This is the area in which you will continue many of the lessons started in Circle Time or other areas. Here are some special ideas you might choose to try when designing your science center.

1. A place for permanent displays. This is where you will put the minimuseum, various collections, the critter cage and similar items.

2. A place for the unique and wonderful. This is a special place where very special objects are displayed, usually one at a time. It can be a small table, a pedestal, or a pretty box which will help to focus attention on the beauty of a crystal, the intricacy of a chambered nautilus, or a stone from the shores of the Arctic Ocean. You, the children, or the parents can supply the objects. We've used everything from a cow's tooth to the first daffodil of spring. You may even wish to bring in a technological treasure such as a computer chip.

3. Science Storage. Open shelves are invaluable. Lower shelves can be used for materials which the children may handle. Higher shelves can store things not currently in use. Materials that are potentially hazardous should be stored out of sight in closed storage. It would be ideal to have a place where experiments and materials could be kept if the table is busy.

We want to encourage independent activity and learning through discovery so we must be sure that the children know where to find the materials they need. Labeling shelves and containers with pictures or words will help keep things orderly and will also build readiness skills. The children will begin to learn to take responsibility for placing objects back in their proper places. By maintaining a neat and attractive center, you are showing the children that the materials and the accompanying work are important and should be handled as such.

SCIENCE SAFETY:
BUILD GOOD HABITS EARLY

Just as children need to be taught the proper way to handle easel painting in the art area, they need to know the best way to use the materials in the science center. Here are some ideas to keep in mind.

1. Most containers should be of metal or plastic. If glass must be used, be sure the children are well supervised. If they need to carry a container, it should be light enough for them to handle easily.

2. Experimental chemicals, even if they are only vinegar and baking soda, should be handled carefully. The containers should be labeled and stored in a special place. ALL CHILDREN SHOULD BE TAUGHT THAT NO UNKNOWN SUBSTANCE SHOULD BE HANDLED WITHOUT ADULT PERMISSION! This is a topic that should be talked over throughout the year with regard to both home and school.

3. While none of the activities in *Mudpies To Magnets* are in any way dangerous, accidents can always happen. Try to anticipate difficulties and always be prepared to postpone an activity if that seems necessary.

4. When new materials are introduced, be sure that all the children know how to handle them and where to store them. It's an easy way to improve your material "survival rate".

RESOURCES

Parents can be valuable resources for teachers. They are usually more than willing to share their talents and experiences with the children. Perhaps they have a hobby or job skill that would spark a child's interest in a science activity. They may have access to materials you need. They may be willing to serve as able-bodied assistants even if they know nothing about the topic at hand. Not only can these contacts help your science program, they can lead to closer relationships with parents. This in turn leads to fuller, more nourishing lives for their children. Don't forget community resources. Scientists, photographers, story tellers, painters, carpenters — the list is endless. Science departments at local high schools and colleges often have people who are willing to take time out to identify a fossil or a feather. They may also be willing to lend models and other items which could be of interest to the children.

Books, periodicals, and science organizations are important resources. A librarian will be able to provide you with many others. You will find that the more you encourage the children to ask questions, the more you will need resources. A collection of inexpensive field guides will allow you to help them "look it up" while the information is fresh. Simple science picture books as well as more advanced texts can often illustrate an idea in a clear way. They may give you information which you can then interpret for the children. Many science magazines, whether for children or adults, have photographs which prove helpful. Let the children see you search for information from a variety of sources and it won't be long before they're searching on their own.

FINDING THE THINGS YOU WILL NEED

*T*his is a list of items that you will need for a successful and active science program. The list can be added to or reduced depending on your needs. Storage of equipment can be a problem. Having a definite science area with adequate shelves will be helpful. Cardboard boxes that can be stacked and labeled will keep everything together.

Take the list below and add any special items which you might need. Prepare a letter for the parents incorporating the list. In addition, prepare a copy of the list for the bulletin board. Make it showy and easy to spot. Be sure to leave room to add new items.

Use the letter on page 17 as a sample.

When something is donated, and you do not need more of the item, cross it off the list. Always be sure to place the name of the donor beside the crossed off item. Add a note thanking the contributors in your monthly newsletter.

Dear parent,

The _____ Center is developing an experimental science program for your child. This program requires using many items that are not presently available in our school. We would like your help in collecting these materials.

If you have materials that are on the following list, put them in a sack with your name and drop them by the office. When we have collected the needed materials and need no more, I will cross that item off the master list that will be posted near the entrance to the office. If a month from now, you find an item on the list, check the master list as we still may not have obtained it. I also will be adding new items to the master list as they are needed. Please, if you have something that is not on the list but you think will be useful, ask me. I am sure most things can be used.

Thank you for your help.

aquarium	shoe boxes	compass
prism	scales	balance
coffee cans	screen wire	tuning forks
screws	plum bobs	mirrors
electric bell	egg timer	kites
iron filings	slinky	telescope
geoboards	egg cartons	sponges
coal	rubber tubing	ping pong balls
wood	potting soil	bottles
batteries	bolts and nuts	switches
levers	wheels/axles	lenses
clocks	dry measuring cups	locks and keys
mechanical junk	barometer	trundle wheel
plastic cups	felt	toy cars
toy boats	dominoes	tag board
nails	file boxes	empty boxes
pulleys	tape measures	hour glass
sun dial	thermometer	metric measuring
rubber bands	candles	rope
rocks	beans and seeds	wool
fur	sand paper	spools
cigar boxes	magnifying glasses	paper punch
old magazines	binoculars	rain gauge
buckets	magnets	tubs
watering can	flower pots	ziploc bag
cooler	gardening tools	stethoscope
small cages	glass jar (gallon)	margarine tubs
yarn	marbles	popsicle sticks
pitcher	funnels	string
spoons	hammer	pliers
screw drivers	ammonia	vinegar
baking soda	salt	baking powder
sugar	rubbing alcohol	epsom salts
liquid soap	dry soap	hand lotion
mineral oil	clear containers	sheet (white)
food coloring	glue	tag board

WHAT TO DO:
SOME THOUGHTS ON TEACHING SCIENCE

*T*he most important component of the curriculum is the teacher. It is his or her role to create a classroom atmosphere which encourages creativity and independence within a safe and secure environment. The teacher should then provide materials and experiences which clarify existing concepts and stretch children toward new ones.

So, what should early childhood science include? Often, the general curriculum centers around seasonal themes, with a heavy emphasis on nature study, neglecting other areas of science. We feel that there should be a more balanced approach. Some of the topics which ought to be considered are:

Matter and Energy — heat, wind, electricity, motors, sound, magnetism, gravity, friction

The Earth — rocks, soil, sand, air, water, metals

The Cosmos — sun, moon, stars, space exploration

Living Things — plants, animals, growth, change, seasons, the human body

To fully absorb ideas in science or any other area, children need the opportunity to repeat activities and experiences several times under many circumstances. They need to explore the same concept in a variety of settings. The children who are told about plants during group time and color a worksheet that says plants need water may retain a little of that information. But the children who handle and discuss droopy dandelions, try to grow lima beans with and without water, and have their attention drawn to a wilted plant so they can notice how it perks up when watered will know, through their own experiences, that plants need water. This is the kind of learning we want to encourage.

"One time only experiences" can leave children with a sense of inadequacy or incompetence rather than a feeling of mastery and pride in accomplishment. They need the chance to repeat activities to allow them to develop real skills. MAGICAL MAGNET MASTERPIECES provides a good example. Given pretty colors of paint and a few minutes, all children can make something nice to take home. However, if they are given the opportunity to work with the materials several times, they will discover that different objects move paint in different ways and will make selections to suit their needs. They will begin to explore color mixing and become aware of the thickness of the paint as a factor that influences their painting. In other words, their skills and knowledge will become more refined. The children will learn for themselves that practice brings improvement. It also brings genuine satisfaction.

It is extremely valuable for children to develop an in-depth understanding of one broad topic. The topic could be magnets, seeds, ramps, making playdough, or anything else. What is important is that children have the feeling of knowing "all about it". They can predict what will happen if variables are changed. They can talk about the topic with another person. They can deal with the subject in many ways. In other words, they have a feeling of being competent, of being an expert. This is important because it carries over to other areas. Once children have experienced the feeling of being good at something, they will have the confidence to pursue being good at something else.

YOUNG CHILDREN AND LEARNING

For children to actively construct their own knowledge, they must have opportunities to manipulate, explore, initiate, and choose. They need the chance to touch, probe, and just play around to find out how things work. Much of the time, the teacher's role is that of a resource person and helper rather than a director. This is not to say that teacher direction is never appropriate. We just want to stress the crucial role self-direction plays in overall growth and learning.

Characteristics of young children which affect science teaching:

1. Most young children find it difficult to remember more than one step or variable at a time.

2. They cannot carry out most operations mentally. They need to manipulate the materials.

3. It is difficult for them to place things in sequence. Trial and error is the most common method children use when placing things in sequence. Since they are often unable to view a collection of objects as a whole, they may group things in several small sequences.

4. They tend to focus on the beginning and end of experiences and miss the changes that occur in the middle.

5. It is difficult for them to see cause and effect relationships. If two things happen at the same time or place, one is seen as the cause of the other whether they are related or not. They are unable to reason logically. Instead make assumptions based on intuition or guesses.

6. They use actions to problem solve and often talk to themselves as they work.

7. Just like adults, they need time to reflect and to absorb ideas in order to fully understand a concept. They may need to accompany this reflection with action.

To summarize, children learn by doing. If the teacher mixes yellow and blue paint and explains that this is how to make green, children may attribute this to "teacher magic". If instead they paint with yellow and blue paints several times, they will be pleased with their own discovery of green and may even remember it. By encouraging curiosity and creativity, you encourage active exploration and learning. Accepting their ideas and challenging them with new ones moves them on to the kind of thinking which has meaning far beyond science facts.

SOME IDEAS ABOUT PLANNING

Activities should be selected to meet children's immediate needs and interests. These will vary with children's ages as well as previous experiences. Isolated facts and concepts are meaningless to young children and are quickly forgotten. Most of the activities in *Mudpies to Magnets* can be used for a variety of purposes. For example, the circle time activity which introduces the water cycle could be used in conjunction with units on weather, farming (how do crops get water), water transportation, and spring ("April Showers . . .") to name a few. Many activities can also be viewed in terms of skill areas such as mathematics or language arts.

We have written the activity chapters to coincide with the most common areas of the curriculum, to encourage the integration of science into the existing program. They are easy to use when planning. Units could be planned around a science topic such as the seasons or plants, or activities could be chosen to be part of a more general unit. A thorough index allows for the selection of activities to coincide with a specific unit. We have included in the index commonly used unit topics and have listed with them activities which might be useful. A unit on transportation could include activities with ramps, wheels, water, and paper airplanes. Halloween is the perfect time for learning about bones. What better time to learn about evaporation than on a hot summer day? As the book's contents become familiar, it will become easy to make science a part of daily experience. The chart on page 22 shows even further possibilities for using the activities.

Here are a few more ideas which have proved helpful in planning:

1. Children should be provided with many opportunities for active, "hands on" involvement with real objects. This is the basis for the later development of more complex thinking.

2. There should be long activity periods which allow children to engage in independent planning and execution of projects.

3. Social interaction should be encouraged so that personal views can be verified or modified.

4. Adult input should be provided on a one-to-one basis or through small groups formed for a specific purpose. Explanations often don't "explain" at all. Instead, they end up cutting off speculation and curiosity. In other words, don't talk too much.

5. When new materials are introduced, it is wise to allow the children some time for exploration. They will be much more willing to follow adult directions if they have already satisfied some of their curiosity.

Activity Chart	EGG CARTON RAINBOWS *Page 94*	BEAT A LEAF *Page 80*	LISTEN TO THE SOUNDS OF THE BODY *Page 114*
MATH SKILLS	Count number of drops added, count shades of color; # of compartments in egg carton.	Count # of leaves; count points or lobes. Make a rough comparison of time required to beat different leaves.	Count parts you can hear, not hear; compare sizes of bodies.
FINE MOTOR DEVELOPMENT	Use of eye dropper; control amount drawn into dropper; coordinate when dropper is at correct compartment and when to squeeze.	Placement of materials to set up activity.	Hold stethoscope correctly; use of crayons.
GROSS MOTOR DEVELOPMENT	Carrying water containers; pouring water, cleaning up; pouring out dirty water.	Beating the leaf to produce a finished product; collecting leaves; move to music like a leaf.	Does exercise affect body sounds?
SOCIAL DEVELOPMENT	Recording their results to affirm their success. Matching someone else's colors. Working with others and sharing results.	Satisfaction of a job well done, creation of a gift to share. Sharing hammers and best leaves to use; experience of gift giving, enjoying the work of others; can be done as a group project; using tools safely.	Appreciation of their bodies. Recognize common characteristics of all bodies.
LANGUAGE AND VOCABULARY DEVELOPMENT	Color words, preposition words. Describing process during activity to teacher and to children. Sharing results; teacher adds new descriptive vocab. Tell a new person how to do the experiment. Tell another how to make a color.	Leaf identification preposition words, colors, shapes, texture descriptive words. Describe a leaf for another person to find. Discuss why some do not work. Read a story or poem about trees or leaves.	Name and talk about body parts. Can they mimic the sounds heard?
CREATIVITY	Choosing colors to make; self directed activity; the magic of color creation.	Choose own leaf and pattern to produce on cloth; can other printing materials be found?	Drawing their own road maps and choosing their own parts to listen.
VISUAL SKILLS	Color ID, shades of colors, match your colors to someone else's.	Follow outline of leaf. Match and sort leaves.	Look at model and draw in body parts on own body outline.
AUDITORY SKILLS	Following oral directions. Loud and soft, noisy and quiet sounds.	Different sounds that body organs make. Sharing sounds as they are discovered. Listening to directions well enough to be able to explain them to another. Comparing animal body sounds to our own.	
MEMORY	Make the same color twice. Remember tomorrow how to make the colors.	Where to find the leaves they used; names of leaves; do the activity independently later.	Duplicate another's road map. Names of body parts.
CAUSE AND EFFECT	Recognize that certain colors always create the same colors.	Do some hammers work better? Do some leaves work better? Do some beating surfaces or fabrics work better?	Recognize that exercise makes some body sounds louder; stethoscope must be properly placed.
DRAWING CONCLUSIONS	Talking about and writing down results of the sessions. Can results be replicated?		
SEQUENCING	Does order matter in color mixing? Make shades of color dark to light; make color spectrum following a model.	Set up materials in proper order. Sequence leaves by size.	Following road map; listen to sounds in order presented.

Developing concepts

Experiences don't always build concepts. What children gain depends on their perceptions, associations, and prior knowledge. However, these activities do build on previous experiences and introduce new ideas.

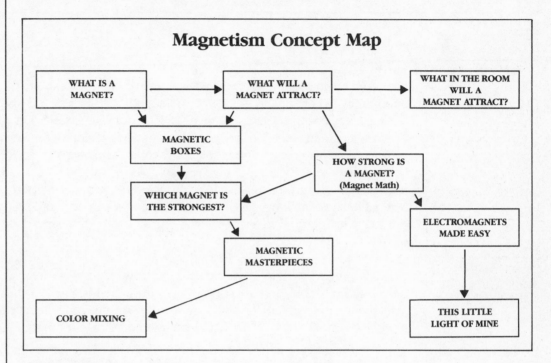

Magnetism Concept Map

Lesson plans

The activities are written in a format which is readily adaptable to a standard lesson plan.

Objective	— Overview
Materials	— Things You Will Need
Preparation	— What to Do
Appraisal	— What to Do
Extension	— Want to Do More

Science skills

There are several key skills which need to be emphasized when working with young children, regardless of the topic being covered. They can learn to experiment with minimal guidance. A simple comment such as, "I see you're having trouble keeping the blocks from falling off the truck. I wonder if there's another way you could try?" can lead children to come up with a variety of options and possibly a solution. They can also learn that not all problems have solutions.

Science activities provide endless opportunities to develop the ability to observe. All the senses can be involved in learning to notice details, identify differences, and recognize similarities. It is important to stress that observation itself is important. We want to develop inquiring minds and perceptive senses, not just children who are storehouses of information.

WANT TO DO MORE: MAKING YOUR OWN SCIENCE KITS

*O*nce you have introduced an activity to the children, it is important to allow them the opportunity to continue to work with the materials and ideas. It is also valuable to extend the experience with related activities. Making your own science kits makes it possible for children to do this independently. With very young children, the kits will be simple collections of materials on one topic for them to freely explore on their own. Older children will benefit greatly from free exploration, but can be challenged with ideas presented by picture cards, drawings, or tapes. These science kits, stored in shoe boxes, resealable bags, small buckets, or other containers, can be kept in the science center. You can then allow the children to work with the kit as they choose to do so, or you may rotate the kits through the center.

As an example, we have described a kit on magnets in some detail. It is based on magnet activities in this book and the concept map illustrated in WHAT TO DO. The materials included are appropriate for a wide range of children. You will have to decide what is useful for your classroom. You'll also want to add things you have found to be valuable.

1. A magnet and a set of objects that will and will not be attracted. (What does a magnet attract?)

2. Assorted magnets and a box of paperclips (are some magnets stronger than others?)

3. MAGNET BOXES page 30

4. Magnetic letters, puzzles and games (commercial products)

5. A picture book about magnets

6. A piece of magnetite (nature's own magnet)

Other kits can be assembled on rocks, dinosaurs, shells, water, simple machines, measurement, or the senses. Think about the topics you cover throughout the year and you'll find that most of them can be enhanced by the use of a related science kit.

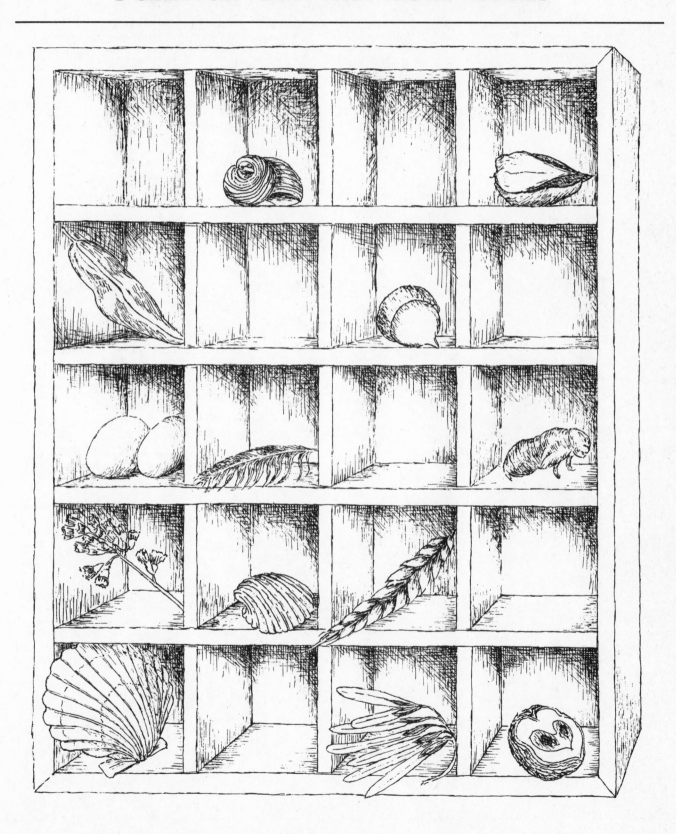

MINIMUSEUMS

A museum gives us the opportunity to take a close and careful look at pieces of our world. It can be a large building in a big city or a place you create yourself. Putting together a private museum gives children the opportunity to see and handle interesting materials. It also is a special place for displaying their own unique finds.

Words you can use

museum
specimen
examine
observe
look
explore
collection
identify
label
name
discover

Things you will need

large shallow cardboard box

24 1/2 pint milk cartons with tops cut off

a collection of objects of interest to you and the children such as:
    rocks
    feathers
    teeth
    arrowheads
    seeds
    shells
    bark
    fur
    fabric
    insects, etc.

What to do

1. Remove the tops of the milk cartons, and place a set of the cartons in your large, shallow box.

2. For greater stability, staple these together.

3. Once the cartons are stapled into the holding container, fill them with the specimens you have collected.

4. Label the specimens. Your labels can be names or pictures.

5. Talk with the children about the items, then allow them to come to the minimuseum to explore and learn.

Want to do more?

Each minimuseum can become a lotto board for a concentration game. Add egg cartons to hold small objects and other boxes for larger things. Clear plastic medicine bottles are good for small, fragile treasures. Leaves can be pressed, dried in the phone book and covered with clear contact paper to save. Rocks and shells are wonderful to use. Sort and classify in some way, i.e. color, texture, shape. Make seasonal, beautiful, hard, soft, twin or triplet, or everyone's favorite thing collections. Involve the children in the identification process by using children's nature books and illustrated field guides. Some children will begin to look things up on their own. But, remember, not everything has to be identified to be enjoyed.

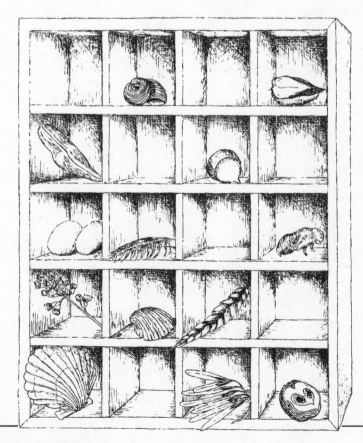

PILL BUG PALACE

One of the most common crustaceans found in North America is the Isopod. It may also be called a roly-poly, pillbug, or sowbug. The Isopod is a crustacean, which means that it is an invertebrate with an external skeleton and jointed appendages. Isopods are easy to collect in the fall when they are in abundance among the fallen leaves they use as food. A good way to collect them is to rake leaves away from the foundation of a building or to look under rocks in damp places. These little creatures are frequently looked upon as "icky" and often fall victim to the stamping feet of adults and children. Helping to find and prepare a home for pillbugs will teach appreciation as well as humane care for this common little creature. That's just what we want!

Words you can use

Isopod
invertebrate
exoskeleton
crustacean
terrestrial
pill bug
roly poly

Things you will need

terrarium (could be made from clear plastic shoebox)

isopods
fallen leaves
sticks and soil

non-breakable collecting containers

What to do

1. Prepare the home for your pillbugs. Place sticks, leaves and soil at the bottom, sloping the soil into hills and valleys. Include a rock, stick, or piece of bark for the Isopods to crawl under. Finally, dampen the soil, as they like a moist but not wet environment.

2. Prepare for a collecting safari by first scouting the school yard or neighborhood to locate pill bugs. Early fall is an excellent collecting time.

3. Go on a pill bug collecting trip with the children. Put the pill bugs in collecting containers as you go.

4. Bring the bugs back to the classroom and gently put them in their home. Put the top on and look at them as they move around to find their niche.

5. Observe for the next several weeks as the pill bugs feed on the leaves and decaying material. Given enough time, the tiny creatures can strip the dried dead leaves to skeletons!

6. The pill bugs may be kept all winter but you will probably want to return them to their natural habitat after observing for a time.

Want to do more?

Observe the pill bugs life cycle. Baby pill bugs look exactly like adults, just smaller. Do they like some leaves better than others? Do they like some places better than others? Do experiments on what pill bugs like and don't like to eat. Shade one side of the cage. Where do they go?

THE GREAT AIR MACHINE RACE

Words you can use

air
blow
squeeze
invisible
force
wind
roll
gust

Things you will need

heavy duty resealable bags

2 sponges for each bag

plastic straws
duct tape

Air takes up space, can move objects, and do work. It is, however, a most difficult concept to explain to young children. So, let's look at air as a mover of things. You still can't see it, but an invisible gust can push an object across the table as surely as your finger. With the air machine your children can feel the force of air, see it move things, and become skilled enough to move obstacles around or hit a target. An extra dividend is the strengthening of hand muscles, so important for school success.

What to do

1. Place the sponges inside the bag. Put the straw between the sponges so that it sticks out of the bag (see illustration). Seal the bag with duct tape. The air machine works by squeezing the sponge which should cause a stream of air to be sent out through the straw.

2. Show the children how to work the machine.

3. Give each child a crayon, acorn, or other "rollable" object which is to be placed on the table and moved by air only.

4. The Great Air Machine race now begins as kids roll their items across the table.

Want to do more?

Along with the air machine, give each child a set of objects with different shapes. Which shapes are easiest to move? Move pieces of similar shape but different weight. Prepare machines with different sizes or numbers of straws. Try to move small plastic and metal cars with wheels to see which (light vs. heavier) is fastest. Make a soap mixture and blow bubbles.

THE MAIN ATTRACTION: MAGNET BOXES

Words you can use

magnets
iron filings
attract

force field (the non-cartoon version)

Things you will need

a shallow box with a clear, plastic lid such as a stationery box, (or a shallow box and heavy plastic wrap)

heavy tape such as duct or book binding tape

magnets

iron filings — these are available from hardware stores who cut thread on iron pipe or from scientific supply companies (see your local yellow pages)

Iron filings are often listed in articles on magnets as an interesting material for children to use. With young children, even the not so young, problems are soon obvious. These sand-sized particles of iron cling to the magnets, spill on the floor, and soon lose their educational value. Magnet boxes allow children to work freely with iron filings and other materials without the hassles. Work with magnets can then become an independent activity, available to children at any time.

What to do

1. It is the adult's job to assemble the magnet boxes. This can be done with or without the children. Place enough iron filings in the box to barely cover the bottom. Cover with the lid or heavy plastic wrap. Seal the box completely with the tape. While you're at it, reinforce the corners. If you have done all this properly, you will have a sturdy, escape-proof box. You may want to make several, depending on the number of children you have as only one child can use it at a time. Play with it a while to discover for yourself what can be done.

2. Show the children how to use the box by moving a magnet across the bottom to make the iron filings move. They look through the top to see the results. Using the magnet on the plastic side is certainly permissible, the results just aren't as dramatic. The kids will soon discover this on their own.

3. After the children have had a chance to thoroughly explore the possibilities of the magnet boxes, they may begin to talk about the pattern created when the magnet is first touched to the bottom of the box. If not, show them. Different magnets produce different designs. Demonstrate with an assortment if possible. Tell the children that this is one type of real force field. It shows the area that is affected by the power of the magnet. Some magnets are more powerful than others and so affect a larger area. If you like, you can make permanent magnet pictures. Use the time tested method of sprinkling filings on sturdy paper, placing the magnet underneath, and spraying the resulting design with clear varnish.

4. The magnet boxes should be available to the children so that the fun and experimentation can continue over an extended period of time. Big ideas need more than one lesson period to be absorbed. The boxes make it easy to give the children that valuable time.

Want to do more?

Vary the amount of iron filings in the boxes. Place other objects in the boxes with or without the filings. You might want to use some things which magnets don't attract. See the index for other magnet ideas.

DANCING DROPPERS

Words you can use

pressure
air
sink
float
rise
fall
up
down

Things you will need

A clear plastic squeeze bottle labels removed filled with water — (a flexible syrup bottle works well)

an eye dropper

You have to see it to believe it! This is one of those age old marvels that takes advantage of the mystery of a scientific principal. It is actually known as a Cartesian Diver and is used to demonstrate air pressure in physics classes. Most people would not consider teaching young children about the principles of air pressure. In theory, it is far beyond their grasp. However, children do not need to understand the laws of physics to enjoy playing with a dancing dropper. In addition, it provides a highly motivating method of providing exercise for children who need stronger hand muscles.

What to do

1. Fill the bottle three quarters full of water.

2. Float an eye dropper in a vertical position in the water by sucking water into the dropper until it floats upright. (It is best to test this in a tall glass before beginning so that you don't have to keep emptying the syrup bottle).

3. After placing the eye dropper into the squeeze bottle, put the top on tightly.

4. Squeeze the bottle and the eye dropper should sink.

5. Allow the children to experiment with the bottle. With the right squeeze on the bottle, the child should be able to hold the eye dropper diver at the bottom of the bottle.

Want to do more?

Use colored water when filling the dropper. This will show how water exchanges in the dropper. Leave the top open and squeeze. What happens? Science note: This Cartesian diver works because you change air pressure in the big bottle. As you squeeze the bottle you decrease the space inside it. This in turn increases the pressure inside the bottle as well. Water is then pushed up inside the dropper which causes it to become heavier and then to sink. Pressure equalization is the cause of it all.

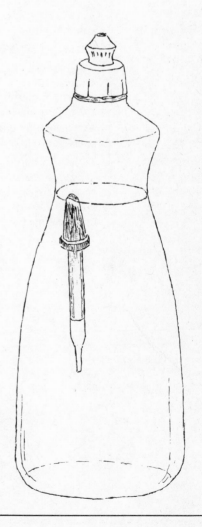

FISH—UP CLOSE AND PERSONAL

Words you can use

mouth
fin
anus
tail
gills
scales
eyes

Things you will need

A goldfish
an aquarium
drawing materials
paper

It is important for all of us to be able to observe, and remember details, a skill which is acquired through practice. This was made particularly obvious several years ago when a group of 3-5 year olds was asked to draw grass. They drew various combinations of green lines and squiggles. They were then taken out to actually look at and talk about grass. The difference in the drawings which they made upon their return to the classroom was amazing. The new pictures included brown and yellow grass, weeds, bumps, rocks, and dirt. Even the youngest had noticed the variations in color. In this activity, observing a fish, the children need plenty of time for looking. The teacher assists by providing the terminology and eliciting descriptive words from the children. The drawings are a way of recording the experience. If drawings are done before and after observing, the teacher and children may be able to see the results of careful observation. The value of this activity is in repetition - with people, animals, plants, anything. You are teaching children to see the world. So now, get on with the fish—up close and personal!

What to do

1. Hand out drawing materials.

2. Ask the children to draw a fish.

3. Place the goldfish, in its bowl, on the science table.

4. As the day progresses each child is to go to the science table to watch the fish. They should observe the movement of the fish through the water. Talk about the fish, encouraging the children to describe what they see. Identify for the children the parts of the fish listed above. Often, having a name for something, even if the name is forgotten later, helps in seeing it as a distinct part.

5. The fish could be fed as the observations proceed so that children may watch the fish eat.

6. After a period of observation and discussion about the fish's physical characteristics, the children should be given drawing materials and asked to draw the goldfish.

7. Show before and after drawings. The difference will amaze everyone. The powers of observation learned through this lesson will be useful in other scientific ventures.

Want to do more?

Observe the behavior of the fish. Add another fish. Does the behavior change? Observe the eating habits as food is placed in the bowl. Discuss what a fish needs to live by comparing it to human needs. Bring in pictures of other fish. How are these fish alike and different?

OH I SEED YOU

Words you can use

seed

seed names

descriptive words such as smooth, shiny, little

Things you will need

Seeds — 3-10 kinds, for example, peas, bean, corn, watermelon, wheat, soybeans, pumpkin, sunflower, milo. (The more sophisticated your group, the more similar the seeds can be).

Plastic bags or small cups,

small paper plate or piece of paper on which to place the seeds for each child.

*A note of caution: seeds from the seed rack at the garden store are often treated with a fungicide and should be avoided! Check with the seed dealer before you buy.

Many activities can be done with seeds. They are easy to obtain in both variety and quantity and thus make a readily available teaching tool. In this lesson the focus is on the children's ability to observe and to communicate those observations. They can work with number, texture, shape, size, and color using just a handful of seeds. Not bad!

What to do

1. Prepare a bag of seeds for each child. The bags should be identical so that all the children will have the same groups of seeds to discuss. For example, you might want to give each child 5 sunflower seeds, 2 pinto beans, 3 pumpkin seeds, 4 wheat seeds, and 1 peach seed.

2. Give each child a bag of seeds and a paper plate.

3. Have the children look at the seeds and share their observations with the group. Very young ones will have only a few remarks while the older children can go on forever. The teacher should list their observations and elicit new ones. Give the children ample time to explore and think, but be careful. It should be fun, not tedious.

4. Select a seed and review its characteristics. Count the seeds.

5. Ask one student to choose a seed and describe it for the rest of the children. As they recognize which one is being described, they should pick it up. Take turns observing and describing.

Want to do more?

Count and add seeds. Use only touch to identify seeds. Give them glue and paper so that they may make a picture from the seeds. Plant the seeds. With very young children, use only one set of seeds which the teacher and children can then examine together. Also, larger seeds will be easier for the young one to handle.

3

SHADOW BOX

Words you can use

shadow
light
image
pattern
up
down
bottom
top
side
center
large
small
big
medium

Things you will need

light source (filmstrip projector, lamp)

large box 45cm x 60 cm (18″ x 24″)

white fabric
figures

box cutter or x-acto knife

This shadow box activity focuses on learning location words that are important to pre-reading. As the child moves the shapes in front of the light source different positions such as top, bottom, and side, take on real meaning because of the boundaries set by the screen. With practice, the children will then be able to transfer to other situations the concepts of direction and spatial positions which they have learned through their play with the shadow box.

What to do

1. Construct a shadow box from a box at least 45cm x 60 cm (18″ x 24″) To do this, open the end of the deepest portion of the box by cutting out the end of the box leaving a 2 cm edge for stability.

2. Tape or staple a piece of white fabric over the entire surface at the end of the box. Turn the box so the open top faces the side. Cut an opening opposite the screen to allow the light to enter. Place your light source in the opening. (see illustration.)

3. Cut out the figure of a person, and fix this figure on the end of a stick.

4. Place the cut-out into the shadow box through the open side. Look at the shape's shadow.

5. Learn how to place the shape into the box so it is right side up.

6. Have a child or the teacher give instructions on where the shadow is to move. i.e. up, down, top, bottom, side, center.

Want to do more?

Create more figures, male, female, children, dogs, birds, other animals. Make a show for the class. Illustrate a story book. Use three dimensional shapes and determine the two dimensional shadows that are created by the shapes.

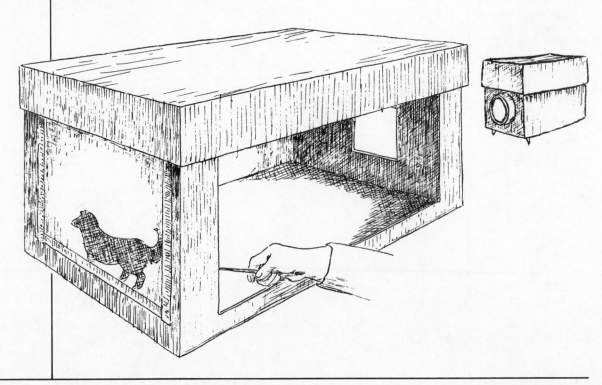

SHAKE, SHAKE, SHAKE

Words you can use

taste
touch
smell
feel
listen
hear
senses
names of body parts
match
different
same
pair
belong
alike

Things you will need

film canisters or darkened bottles

objects to place in the containers — 3 containers make a set — 2 that match and 1 that doesn't.

Examples of sets are: 2 marbles and 1 rock (sight), 2 containers almost filled with salt and a quarter full of sugar (taste), 2 small circles of sandpaper and a penny (touch), 2 cloves and 1 cinnamon stick (smell).

It's time for a new twist on the old shake and match game. This activity gets all the senses involved. It can begin as a simple "which one doesn't belong" game with the children matching by sound, taste, smell, or texture. As the children work with the materials and become more skillful, they can learn to play more complex games with the same materials. In the process, they develop their sensory, discrimination, and memory skills.

What to do

1. Place the sets of objects in canisters, leaving all containers accessible to the children. Getting the tops off to check the answers may be difficult for some.

2. Each container is labeled on the bottom by the sense, other than sound, which can be used to identify its contents. These labels can be taped or glued on the container (see illustration). This will serve as a self check — Put all the smells together and one will not match.

3. The children are to shake the containers and to determine by sound which two match or which one doesn't belong. Then they may open the containers and use their other senses to see if they are right. Less experienced children will need to begin with sets of three containers. More may be added as their skills improve.

Want to do more?

Take off the labels and have the children determine the sense used. Have children make up new sets. Remove a sense, e.g., Can you tell sugar from salt without taste?

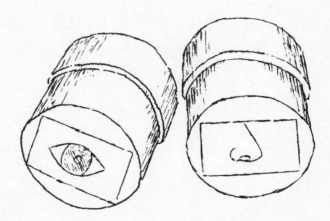

TOUCHY FEELY BOX

The mystery box as an activity is found in many science centers. This idea is just another twist to learning to identify things by touch. It goes one step further by adding a communication dimension to the find and feel "touch-feely" box.

Words you can use

touch
hard
soft

and other descriptive words

Things you will need

three matching sets of various objects such as nuts, feathers, pinecones, sticks, leaves, shells, and rocks

What to do

1. Build a touch box such as the one suggested here. (see illustration) The box should have 2 openings so that two children may work together. Attach old socks over the openings so hands can slip into the box and not be seen.

2. Place 2 sets of items in the box. Also place a set in sight of the two participants.

3. Have a child reach in and describe one of the objects in the box by touch. The child can look at the visible objects, using the sense of sight to help support his or her touch descriptions.

4. As one child describes the object, the other child is to find that object in the box by using the sense of touch. Both of them pull out their shapes. Do they match? How are they similar and/or different? Look at any incorrect shapes, review the characteristics described, and put them back. Try again.

5. The fun of this touch game is obvious. Hands touching and sharing secret shapes are wonderful. The verbal exchange can serve to teach descriptive attributes and touch words with instant reviews by the teacher and a self correcting mode built into the game.

Want to do more?

Choose more touch words: hard-soft, warm-cold, smooth-rough. Make up many mystery boxes and have the children match boxes containing like objects. For young children, place an object on top of the box and have them reach inside to find the match.

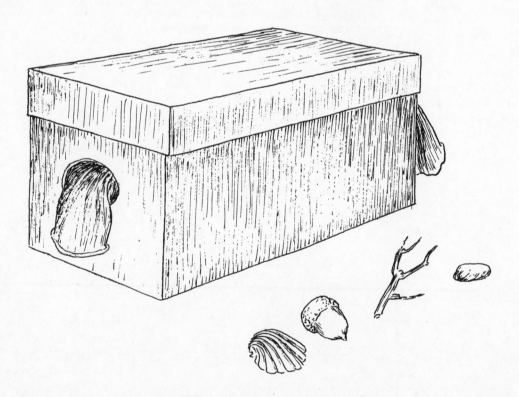

BIG DIPPER, LITTLE DIPPER
EVERYONE'S A STAR

Words you can use

stars
night
sky
planets
constellation
Big Dipper

Things you will need

toilet paper rolls for each child

black construction paper

a pencil

a star chart or constellation chart

a water dipper or ladle

The stars are fascinating to young children. They sing about them, hear stories about them, and gaze at them in the evening sky. "Twinkle, Twinkle, Little Star" is among the first songs children learn and yet stars are hard to teach about because we cannot reach out and touch them. A simple "star machine" familiarizes the children with the Big Dipper. It gives them a starting point from which to continue to explore and learn about those twinkling jewels in the heavens.

What to do

1. Talk with the children about stars. Show pictures of constellations and how ancient people looked at the stars and saw shapes of animals and people in them.

2. If this activity is done in winter the class can go out to see the first stars of evening or the last of morning. Around December 21 are the shortest days. The morning and evening stars, however, are planets, not stars. The light of planets is strong and continuous while stars twinkle.

3. Now that the topic is introduced, prepare a star making machine for each child. You may choose from the many constellations, but the easiest to find in any northern sky is the Big Dipper (or Big Bear) constellation.

4. Cut out a piece of black paper following the pattern illustrated.

5. Glue the black construction paper to the end of the toilet paper roll. Allow one day to dry.

6. With a sharp pencil punch the Big Dipper design into each of the tubes. Hold this up to the light and look through it to see your constellation.

7. Because young children may not have used a dipper, bring one for them to see. Let them use it to get a drink. Show how the dipper from which you drink and the star dipper are alike.

8. Now plan for an outside Big Dipper hunt. Because it will need to be done at night, you may want to send the star machine home with an explanatory note. This allows the parents to be involved in their children's learning experiences and bridges the gap between home and school.

Want to do more?

Use oatmeal containers or snack cans to make a star generator for use on a ceiling or blackboard. Construct a design similar to the smaller Big Dipper rolls using the larger container as a projector. Again use a sharp pencil or pen to create the constellations. Make the holes small at first, enlarging them if more light is needed. Turn out the lights and put a flashlight in the container. Voila! Stars on the ceiling. Match the constellations to stories you might have available. Remember, each of the Zodiac signs is a constellation. A monthly star locator can be found in the journal, Science and Children. Use it to find out which stars or planets are most visible, as well as their locations in the sky.

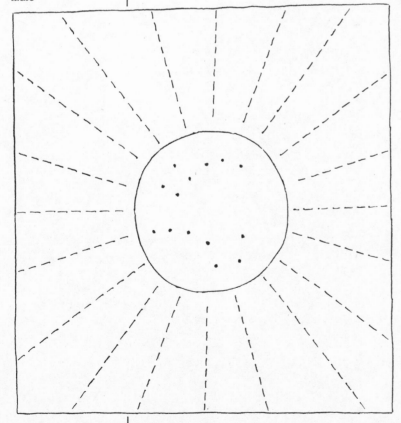

CLING TO ME

Word you can use

static
electricity
charge
electrons
shock

Things you will need

salt/pepper
bits of styrofoam
puffed rice

pairs of clear plastic
tops from deli food

containers
airplane glue
piece of fur
nylon

Every object has extra electrons present on its surface. Electrons are charged particles that, when treated correctly, flow to form electricity. With the right conditions they can be increased on a body or object and can be present in numbers sufficient to cause static electricity. With the materials in this activity, your children can create the conditions for a container to be supercharged by static electricity.

What to do

1. It is the teacher's job to prepare the materials for this activity. Begin with one pair of lids. Place about 1/2 teaspoon each of salt and pepper in one lid. Place a line of airplane glue around the rim of the other. Put the lids together and allow them to dry. When dry, the salt and pepper should move freely and the container should be completely sealed. If it leaks, patch with a little glue.

2. Make several more containers filling each with a small amount of the materials listed above. Use only one substance per container.

3. When the containers are dry, rub one with the fur or nylon. Static electricity will be created inside on the objects and they will dance around. In humid weather the reaction is not as great.

4. Touch the surface. The objects cling to your finger and will move in response to your movements.

5. Place the containers on the science table for the children to use independently. What else can they think of to put in the static boxes? Some ideas will work and some won't, but all are worth a try.

Want to do more?

Try using a rubber comb or glass rod to touch the containers. Rub the surfaces of things with nylon or fur to see if they will attract or cling. Also, try using a clothes drier fabric softener sheet.

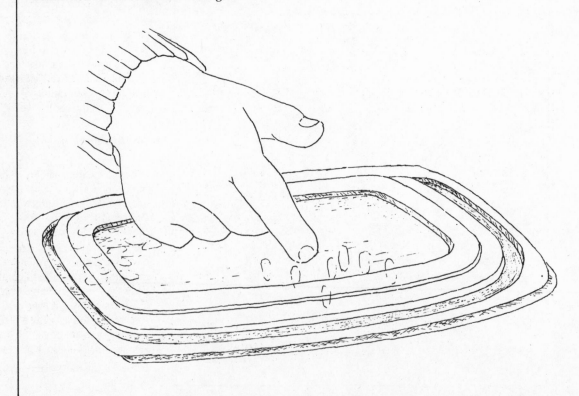

PUT A ROCK TO BED

Words you can use

mineral
rock
properties
texture
appearance
shiny
layered
old
color
Earth Science
geologist
strata

Things you will need

rocks which the children have collected

shoeboxes

materials or pictures to make dioramas of various environments such as the seashore, woodlands, or a stream bed

How many of us have taken a trip to the mountains, the seashore, the river, the creek, or the park and picked up a rock as a remembrance? Most often it ends up in a box somewhere which eventually is thrown away. Why not bring the rocks out of the boxes and put them to use? Instead of wasting a resource naturally attractive to children, use their interest to help them become more adept at observing, classifying, and describing.

What to do

1. Prepare the shoeboxes by turning them on their sides and using materials, pictures, or both to simulate the settings for your rocks. For example, if you have rocks from the Grand Canyon, you could glue a picture of the canyon in the back of the shoebox as a background for the scene and glue sand or brown paper in the box for the foreground. A woodland scene could have a picture of trees as background with dried grass and dirt for the "floor". Use your imagination to create the proper settings for the rocks you have. (see illustration)

2. Tell the children that one way geologists identify rocks is by the location in which they are found. The environment affects rocks. River rocks are tumbled by the water and have few sharp edges. Rocks from a quarry are rough because they have been blasted loose.

3. Talk about the rocks the children have brought to share. Where were they found? Why did they want to keep them? What words can they think of to tell what the rocks look like? Place the rocks in the appropriate scenes. Geologists use the term bed when referring to the strata in which a rock is found. Are there rocks which don't have the right bed? Make one.

4. Place the rocks and boxes in the science area so that the children can continue to use them. They may want to add other materials to the dioramas or create new ones of their own.

Want to do more?

How many ways can your rocks be grouped or classified? Compare them to commercial rock collection cards. Can they find a match? Visit a geology display or a lapidary shop.

PUT THEM IN A ROW

Classification has many facets, one of which is taught in this lesson requiring children to place objects in order. The use of natural objects allows children to become familiar with them as they do the ordering. Changing the objects, increasing the number to be ordered or counting the number of moves, causes the child to think ahead before moving.

What to do

1. Prepare a game board. The size should depend on the age and skills of the children. (see illustration)

2. Place sets of objects on the board so each row is filled with similar objects. In a 9 square board you would have 3 sets of three.

3. Show a child the board set up. Give the child another board, and ask him or her to duplicate the first board with another set of identical items.

4. A more complex task would be to show the child an ordered set. Remove the objects from the board and have the child put the items back in sequence.

5. Show a child a set up. Remove one object, so that there is now only one empty space on the board. Mix the remaining items by moving each item to a different space.

6. Now, one move at a time have the child reorder the objects as they were before the mixing. Moving can only be done into an open square.

Want to do more?

Let the children collect things to make their own game boards. Have them set up a board for a friend. As skill increases, try larger game boards or working more from memory. Use an abacus to count the number of moves.

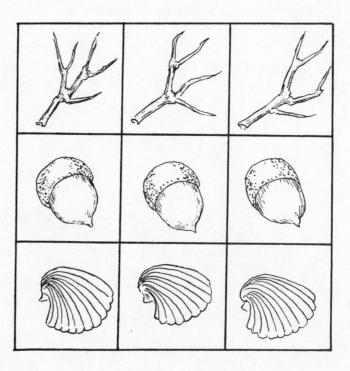

REAL PUZZLES

4

Words you can use

apart
together
fasten
unfasten
screw
unscrew
battery
spring
turn
other words as
needed for the
objects at hand

Things you will need

action-oriented
objects such as
flashlights, padlocks
and keys, latches and
other fasteners

tongs and tweezers
sifters
pulleys
paper punchers
screw lid jars
hand egg beater
clocks

ballpoint pen (for
older children only
because of smaller
parts)

tool sets — hammer
and nails,
screwdriver and
screws, nuts and
bolts and wrench
and pliers

wood to use as
needed

anything else which
might be interesting
to children

The world is full of things to take apart and put together. A collection of common household items for children to explore freely, inside and out, allows them the satisfaction of figuring out how real things work. It also gives them a sense of control and makes the world a little less mysterious. Such a collection can offer a wealth of learning that is almost all child-directed. You can begin with something as simple as a flashlight. How refreshing!

What to do

1. What to do will vary somewhat depending on what objects are being used. As an example, we will consider flashlights, using one small and one average sized flashlight.

2. Show the children the flashlights. Turn the lights out and test them. You may want to talk about uses, other kinds of flashlights, etc. Compare the sizes and talk about similarities and differences.

3. Take the flashlights apart one at a time. As you take them apart, show how the springs make them jump apart so the children won't be surprised when it happens to them. This is an important part of the demonstration as we don't want the children to feel as if they've broken something. Name the components as you work. If you don't know the real name of a part, say so. Lay the parts out so the children can compare the two flashlights.

4. Put the flashlights back together, showing them what happens when the batteries are put in incorrectly. For very young children you may want to use the small flashlights with only one battery.

Let the children know that it may take them a few tries to figure out how to put it back together, just as sometimes it takes awhile to figure out a picture puzzle. If they get really stuck, perhaps a friend can help them.

5. The flashlights can now be made available for use at the science table or puzzle area. You will have to decide whether you want to have only one type of "puzzle" out at a time, or several. Things such as an assortment of locks and keys need no formal introduction and can be used at any time. Other things will require a discussion similar to the one for flashlights. Gradually, a collection can be accumulated which allows the children to explore a variety of mechanisms and will also develop visual memory and discrimination, fine motor skills, and problem solving.

Want to do more?

Have the children bring in their own contributions to the REAL PUZZLE area. Visit a repair shop where people are working on "real puzzles."

SEED POWER

Geologists state that soil is formed by the roots of plants which break down rocks by slow, steady pressure. Wind and water also affect rock, forming soil, but this is a very slow process and is difficult to show to children. SEED POWER serves to demonstrate on a small scale just how powerful the simple sprouting of a seed can be.

Words you can use

plant
growth
smother
prevent
surfaces
seeds
germinate
sprout
power

Things you will need

small, clear plastic containers

plaster of paris
water
lima bean seeds
potting soil

What to do

1. Fill 2 clear plastic containers half full of potting soil or sand.

2. Plant 3 lima bean seeds in one container.

3. Water until moist, but not soaked.

4. Place 3 lima beans on top of the soil in the second container.

5. Mix plaster of paris and water. Make it runny.

6. Pour a thin layer of plaster of paris over the beans in container two. Use just enough to cover them.

7. The seeds must be kept moist. Water them every day.

8. How do you think this plaster of paris cover will affect the growth of the seeds? Will it smother them or do you think they will grow? Record the children's predictions.

9. Observe the containers for 2 weeks and compare. What happens to the seeds? What do you think happens to plants that are covered by blacktop or concrete to make surfaces for parking lots and playgrounds?

Want to do more?

Try other seeds. Are some stronger than others? Take a walk and look for things growing through cracks.

PLASTER

SOIL

TEXTURE COLLAGE: TAKE YOUR FINGERS FOR A WALK

Words you can use

rough
smooth
collage
hard
soft
texture
slick
bumpy

and any other descriptive words

Things you will need

leaves
pinecones
wood
rocks
and other nature walk treasures

a variety of materials of different textures such as cotton balls, plastic, sand, and cloth

Young children are constantly using their sense of touch. It is one of their tools for exploring and evaluating each new experience. Our texture finger walk helps children focus on the sense of touch and encourages the development of descriptive language as they talk about their "journey". Tactile discrimination improves as children learn to "walk down the road" in search of a particular texture. Their fingers will never feel the same again!

What to do

1. The adult should collect the items for the texture collage.

2. On a piece of tagboard, or heavy cardboard, draw a path and a series of garden areas.

3. On the path area spread a thin layer of glue and sprinkle sand on the glue. You have made a rough road.

4. Now fill in each garden area by gluing a group of identical objects on the board. As you add the objects to the collage, discuss the texture of each. A forest of pine cones or a bed of cotton have definite textures and will be remembered as smooth or rough, but they may also have other attributes. Discuss the possibilities.

5. Complete your texture collage and allow it to dry. The collage will be a series of texture gardens connected by the rough road. (see illustration)

6. The teacher asks one child to walk down the road with his or her fingers, eyes open. Discuss the rough road, the smooth stones, the hard, smooth, mirror lake, etc., as the child "walks" through the collage.

7. Have another child walk down the rough road to the soft cotton patch and describe it, or have the child tell about another garden spot on the collage.

8. Finally, blindfold a child and let him or her follow the path through the texture collage. Talk about what is felt along the way. Encourage creative use of language by asking the children to describe what their fingers are feeling. With some children you may want to introduce additional descriptive words.

9. Place the collage in the science center for free play.

Want to do more?

Have the children make up stories about the spots on the collage as they take their trips. Add descriptive words written on 3 x 5 cards to the texture areas. Develop a list of describer words for each texture garden area. A pine forest may be prickly, sharp, hard, rough, tall, and round.

SOUND TRAVELER

Words you can use

sound
transfer
tuning fork
ear
receiver
loud
soft
listen

Things you will need

2 tuning forks —
one high pitch, one
low pitch

5 or 6 items of equal
length such as: a
piece of Styrofoam, a
wooden block, a
piece of heavy
plastic

a piece of aluminum
or iron

a piece of cardboard

a hollow tube

any other materials
you may have

Sound travels through different objects at different rates. It is upon this principle that scientists develop new materials to transmit information for computers and communication lines. Each material has properties that make sound transference occur differently. This experiment asks the children to sort objects according to their ability to transfer sound. If you want to keep sound down you will choose a different material than if you want to transmit sound. For SOUND TRAVELER have the children imagine that they are choosing some materials to make a sound proof room and some to make a wonderful new telephone.

What to do

1. Show the children how to use the tuning fork by striking the fork and placing the end on the table.

2. Have them put an ear on the table to hear the sound being transmitted.

3. Explain that the sound is transmitted from the fork through the table to their ears. The tuning fork makes the sound. It is transmitted through the wooden table and is received by the ear.

4. Have two children work together. One hits the fork on the table and holds it to the object to be tested. The other holds the object to his or her ear and listens. Then they switch tasks.

5. As each object is tested, the children should place it in one of two designated spots, one for good sound travelers and one for poor.

CAUTION: DO NOT USE THE TUNING FORK DIRECTLY AGAINST THE HEAD OR EAR BONES. PAIN OR INJURY COULD RESULT!

Want to do more?

Bring in a picture of the ear to show how sound is received. Older children may be able to put the objects in order from best to worst sound travelers. Try CALL ME as a related activity.

BUILDING WITH SCIENCE: CONSTRUCTION AND MEASUREMENT

BALANCING TOYS

2

Words you can use

balance
weights
center
middle
gravity
equal

Things you will need

peg-type wooden clothes pin

30 to 45 centimeters of wire

large metal washers or old keys for weights

One way to teach about balance is to use a scale. Another meaning of balance is more similar to the tightwire or balance beam. This activity uses the idea of creating a toy to teach balancing concepts. It shows how an object that has little balancing ability can be manipulated so that it can be perched on the tiniest of points. The fine motor skills used to create balance items and to finally balance them may be equally important as you pursue this activity.

What to do

1. Try to balance the clothes pin upright on the end of your finger for the children. Let them try it, too. Not too easy, right? Now let's try it another way using gravity to help us.

2. Center the wire and wrap it a few times around the base of clothes pin so that there is about the same amount on each side. As you work, talk about what you are doing, saying things like, "I'm going to fold the wire and match the ends so I can find it's middle. For our toy to work, we need equal amounts of wire on each side of the clothes pin." Bend the wire to attach a washer on each side (see illustration). Put the clothes pin on a child's finger and bend the wires to adjust it until it balances upright.

3. Encourage the children to try balancing the toy in different ways. Who can balance it on a knee, a thumb, or a head? Place the balancing toy in the science area for independent explorations.

Want to do more?

Make several balancing toys, then play music and have a balancing dance. Bring in other balancing toys for children to see and/or use. Show them a gyroscope and balance it on a string. Make a toy with heavier wire and a sturdy hook on each end so the children can experiment with changing weights (an old coat hanger works well). Using a balance scale and a table top seesaw made of blocks, allow them to discover more about balance and weight independently. Try balancing a potato on your hand by sticking a fork in each side.

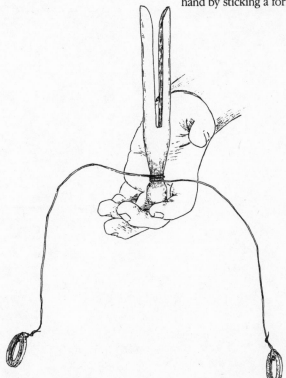

PULLEY INTO LINE

Words you can use

pulley
belt
turn
crank
rotate

Things you will need

3 to 5 thread spools (preferably wooden)

long thin rubber bands

nails

a piece of 3/4 in. plywood or particle board 25 to 30 cm square

Often we grow into adulthood knowing very little about pulleys. We use them in elevators, cars, and other equipment and yet many of us are not really familiar with their function or purpose. By building a simple apparatus which demonstrates pulley function, we can help the children to understand how pulleys work. This can lead to making actual working pulleys for lifting building blocks or some other essential operation. Besides that, it's fun to turn the crank and make everything move at once!

What to do

1. Place the spools on the plywood in a design similar to the one illustrated. Nail the spools in place so they turn easily. With a magic marker place an arrow on top of each spool. This mark will help the children to see which way the spools turn (see illustration). Hammering a nail into one of the spools to serve as a crank also makes the spools turn more easily.

2. Have a child place rubber bands over the spools as shown. Turn one spool and watch the others turn.

3. Experiment with other rubber band arrangements and see what happens.

Want to do more?

Have the experimenters determine the direction the arrows turn when 2 spools are used. Then add another rubber band to a third spool, does this spool turn in the same direction? Twist one rubber band. What now? Attach colored designs to the tops of the spools. How do they change when the spools turn? Turn over an upright vacuum cleaner, remove the plate and look at the belt on the bottom. What does it do to help the vacuum cleaner work? Bring in real pulleys and show how to use them. Can the children put them to use?

CAN I MAKE A SHAPE?

3

Words you can use

shape words such as rectangle or rectangular, triangle, circle, cylinder, square, cube, area

Things you will need

tag board or old file folder

index cards

soft drink cans with holes taped over with duct or carpet tape to protect little fingers

cardboard cases to hold the cans for storage

permanent markers ruler or straight edge

We usually think of volume and area as higher level math skills, and in terms of pencil and paper work they are. Get rid of the pencil and switch to cans and you can create a valuable learning experience for young children. In addition to getting them to think and problem solve, the can puzzles are great for developing visual perception and fine motor skills. Besides, they're fun to use for building just about anything! This activity provides a concrete basis for the complex idea that volume is a three-dimensional representation of an area.

What to do

1. Collect and clean several cases of soda cans. Allow them to dry. Tape the holes. You may want to select or assemble a variety of soda types. This will encourage some classifying or grouping as the designs are "built".

2. On a piece of tag board, set out the cans in shapes of your choice. When the shape has been made with the cans, trace around it using a ruler or masking tape to create the shape with straight lines. Make cards using a variety of shapes.

3. Lay the card on the floor and have the children fill it with soda cans.

4. Can the children now create an identical shape without the card?

5. Continue with the remaining cards. Once the children have mastered the process, the materials can be placed in the classroom for independent use.

Want to do more?

Have the children create their own puzzle cards for friends. Have three-dimensional objects to match to the shapes made. Play shape games by drawing a card and rolling dice to determine the amount of cans allowed each roll. Count the cans needed to make each shape. Which cards need the most cans? The least? What is the smallest square you can make? The largest? Make shapes free form without traced designs.

NEWSPAPER CONSTRUCTION

Words you can use

build
construct
shape
angle
strength
architect
plan
site

Things you will need

newspaper
tape

Children love to build things they can play in. Instead of expensive hollow blocks, roll newspapers into logs for life-size construction. Children build with them for hours, creating increasingly complex tunnels, houses, and the ever-popular hideout. They will experience balance, cause and effect, structure strength, angles, curves, and shapes. You'll be impressed with what you see.

What to do

1. Take two sheets of newspaper and roll into a tight roll. Tape with masking tape to prevent unrolling — a small piece or two is all that is needed. The completed roll is 3 to 5 cm in diameter. Let the children help.

2. Repeat the above procedure until you have 50 to 500 newspaper logs. (Believe us — this doesn't take as long as you think!)

3. Let the children construct anything they want — a tower, a house, a rocket ship, a bus, a train, an igloo, a fence. Some structures will be self-supporting, others will need the help of props or tape.

Want to do more?

Supplement newspaper logs with other building materials to create new and interesting constructions. Open sheets of newspaper, blankets, chairs, card tables, and coffee tables can provide materials for expanding this activity throughout the room. Let the children play architect. The younger children can talk about plans and ideas as the older ones sketch ideas on paper. Design a house for the guinea pig. Visit a construction site. Discuss blueprints to show what grownups do when they are engaged in similar activities. Discuss cause and effect, e.g. Our building keeps falling down! Why? How can we build it so it won't fall down?

RAMPIN' IT

The block area of the learning center provides the materials, and the children's own toy cars provide the motivation to make this activity a successful one. Have the children bring their toy cars and assorted mobile toys to school, add the skills for creating appropriate ramps and the race is on. But it is not easy to produce a good racing ramp. Some will be too low, some too high, and some, after a bit of experimenting, will be just right. Then it is time to test the track with different vehicles and this is where another set of experiments begins.

Words you can use

ramp
change
fastest
slowest
experiment
height
distance
acceleration
friction
speed
force
heavier
lighter
mass

Things you will need

blocks

small cars and other vehicles

books

board — at least 20 cm (8") wide (back of wallpaper sample book works well)

What to do

1. In the block area, or another space where cars can roll freely, show the children how to build a ramp. To begin with, use the board and just one block. Let those participating roll their cars down the ramp. Show them how to hold them at the top of the ramp and let go without a push. You want to see how far the ramp makes them go without our help. After a few trials, the children will probably begin to compare the cars for speed. Explore this with them, asking "Which do you think is our fastest car? Our slowest?" Stressing which is the class's "best" will help limit the "my car is better" talk.

2. Ask how the ramp could be changed to make the cars travel farther. Let them experiment. They may be cautious types who add on one block at a time. They may add as many blocks as possible. Encourage problem solving. For example, the ramp is so high that the board keeps slipping off. What can we do to keep this from happening? (One group of threes tried to tape it at the bottom and prop it with chairs before deciding to take turns holding it. A group of fives just took the top block off, saying "that's as high as it goes!") Again, as they build, encourage trial runs with the cars to compare distance and/or speed.

3. Some children may want to do formal trials with the ramp at various heights. The distance the cars travel can be marked on the floor with tape so that comparisons can be made. What is the best ramp for making cars go farthest? It is not necessarily the highest. You'll find that if the ramp is too high the cars will crash or veer off to the side.

4. Write about and/or draw a design for the ideal ramp. In other words, the children have conducted an experiment, and made several trials. What are their conclusions? With the results of their experiment, they will know how to build a great car ramp every time.

Want to do more?

Use other materials for ramp building such as different boards or a tube. What else can the ramp be used for? Have the children collect objects which roll or don't roll, using the ramp to test their predictions. Place the ramp on a checkered table cloth. How many squares does each car travel?

CALL ME

Sound travels at different speeds as it passes through materials other than air. This activity gives the children a chance to see how sound is conducted through a variety of substances.

What to do

1. Make a string telephone by removing one lid from each of two tin cans. Punch a small hole in the center of the remaining lid of each can. Thread a string into the hole from the outside of the can. Tie each end of the string in several knots to keep it from coming out of the can as it is pulled taut.

2. Have two children each take a can and gently pull the cans apart until the strings are taut.

3. One child places the can over his mouth and talks while the other child listens, holding his can over his ear.

4. How is the sound moving from one can to the other?

5. Use metal wire in another phone. Remember that the string or wire must be taut. Are the sounds different?

6. Look at telephone wires inside and outdoors.

Want to do more?

Discuss the use of the telephone, emphasizing telephone manners and emergency procedures. Visit a telephone office and observe a switch board being used. Bring out a toy telephone for use. Talk about telephones without wires. Find an old telephone to use as a REAL PUZZLE.

ROLLING, ROLLING, ROLLING

Words you can use

inclined plane
roll
round
flat
bottom
test
predict
ramp

Things you will need

a collection of objects to test on the inclined plane

a plank or board for an inclined plane

blocks or other objects to prop it up

The inclined plane or ramp is a tool used to study the force and energy of a rolling body. It is also a surface for marbles or other things to roll down. Children can easily learn that certain objects roll or don't roll but the inclined plane offers a tool to really explore which objects roll best.

What to do

1. Give the children a group of selected objects some of which will roll or can be made to roll, such as a pencil, ball, crayon, round block, and some objects which do not roll.

2. Have them predict their rolling ability and divide them into three piles.
    1. will roll
    2. will not roll
    3. will roll if placed right
3. Set up the inclined plane (see illustration).

4. Have the children check their predictions by trying to roll the objects.

5. Try each of the objects that do not roll to see if it will roll if it's position is changed. A pencil will roll if placed one way but not another.

6. Allow the children to predict and then experiment with classroom objects to determine whether they will or will not roll.

Want to do more?

Raise or lower the inclined plane. What changes? Measure the distance that various objects roll. Vary the inclined plane's height and see if it's height affects the distance rolled. Place various surfaces on the inclined plane to check their affect on rolling, for example: sandpaper, cloth, or a rubber bath mat. Make a written record of your findings using pictures, words, or both.

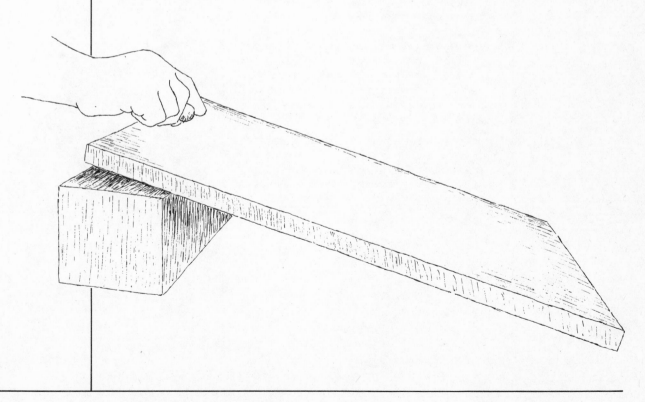

CAVE IN A BOX

Words you can use

freeze
temperature
cave
melt
stalactite
stalagmite
icicle
imagine
pretend

Things you will need

eye dropper
food coloring
water
thick cotton string
small cardboard box

The cold days of winter cause most teachers to draw back into the shell of their classroom to await the warmth of spring. Some activities do, however, require winter's cold. This icicle activity is one of those. It creates a cave formations like those found underground. The ice grows one drop at a time to form simulations of stalactites and stalagmites. Patience and cold weather will reward you with your own cave to explore.

What to do

1. Build a cardboard box cave so that it can be attached to your window and retrieved on the coldest days of winter. Because you will be making your own icicles, your location must be a shady one, and since you will have to add water frequently, it should also be easily accessible.

2. Make a hole in the top of the box about 5 cm (2 in.) across. Tie the heavy cotton string to a stick, and hang the string through the opening until it is just above the bottom. This will serve as a wick and will make your icicle form much faster.

3. On one of your coldest days, begin to form an icicle by dripping water down the string a few drops at a time.

4. As the icicle builds up, talk with the children about how stalactites form from the ceiling of caves as the water, rich in minerals, drips down in one spot. As it flows and evaporates, it leaves its mineral deposits to form the features of the cave. If you have pictures of caves, share them with the children. They may have information of their own to add, too. As you continue to build the stalactite, add food coloring to the water. This simulates different mineral changes in the dripping water.

5. Just as your icicle forms over a long period of time, so the cave requires thousands, even millions of years to build. While the children may not relate to millions of years they will see how long, doing it just a drop at a time, it takes to build their icicle.

6. Some of the water will drop to the bottom of the carton and a formation will appear. This is like a stalagmite.

7. If you have enough time and can cause the stalactite and stalagmite to meet they form, in cave language, a column.

Want to do more?

Read a book on caves. Visit a cave. Make a classroom cave and talk about cave-dwelling animals. See slides or movies of a cave. Make up a story about your cave. Try a freezer for this activity.

DINOSAUR DEN

Words you can use

dinosaur
dinosaur names
cave
home
how many
guess
size
build
construct
plan

comparative words
like big, bigger, etc.

Things you will need

a set of dinosaurs
(check your local toy
store, or sets in scale
can be purchased
from educational
supply catalogs)

rocks — flat river
rocks are wonderful

This activity looks at a very popular subject from a mathematical angle. How many rocks does it take to build a dinosaur den that's not too little, not too big, but just the right size? Children use informal measurement skills to select the number of rocks needed for their cave. With practice, they become increasingly accurate. In the meantime, they refine motor skills and learn a little more about dinosaurs.

What to do

1. Give a dinosaur and some rocks to the child. The objective is to build a cave for the dinosaur. The cave must be big enough for the dinosaur to hide in, but not big enough for another one to squeeze in with it.

2. When that cave has been made, hand the builder another dinosaur. The project is to create a cave for the two of them. The second dinosaur selected should be much larger than the first. Now you have to make a cave big enough for two dinosaurs. An adult should serve as a banker for the rocks by asking how many more rocks will be needed to make the new den. Count the rocks out, "1, 2, 3, . . . 10. Is this enough or too many? Tell me when to stop. 11 . . . 14. If you need more, come back." With experience, their estimates will become more accurate.

3. When the new cave is made, discuss the problems involved in the making of it. Discuss how they knew what to use and how to build walls and a ceiling.

Want to do more?

Add more dinosaurs. Predict the number of rocks needed to house four more dinosaurs or ones of differing sizes. Make permanent cave displays by gluing rocks together. This might be the home for the dinosaurs when they're not being used. Bring in books and pictures about dinosaurs for independent exploration.

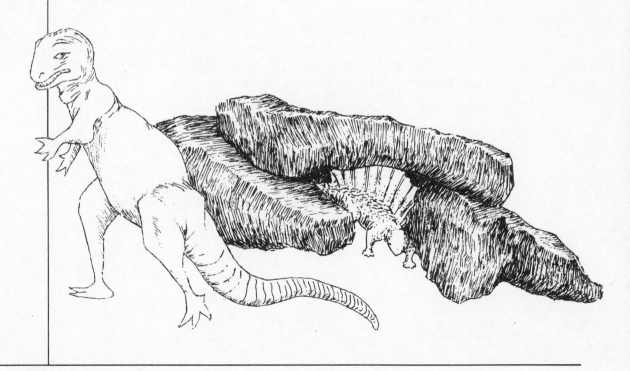

TURNING MUD PIES INTO HOUSES

Words you can use

solid
liquid
evaporation
mix
mixture
adobe
straw
construct

Things you will need

empty pint milk cartons trimmed to about 2cm (1 inch) high

dirt (with clay base helps)

dried straw or grass from the yard

water

large tub for mixing

In times long past, house builders throughout the world discovered that soil mixed with straw and water would, with the sun's help, harden into bricks. These bricks could then be used to build long lasting homes. This technique is still used today and can be replicated in the classroom. Aside from the fun of approved mud play, the children learn about evaporation, building construction, and the creative use of natural resources.

What to do

1. In the mixing tub, mix the soil with the water until it is the consistency of pancake batter. Add the dried grass clippings or straw. It will pour better if the straw is cut into small pieces before mixing.

2. As you mix, talk about the importance of the liquid, water, as a mixing agent and that dirt and water can each be poured. Why do you mix dirt and grass? The grass holds dirt together.

3. Where does the water go? Place a plastic quart bag over one carton of adobe. Water should collect at the top of the bag showing it escaped the mud via evaporation.

4. Place a similar bag, though not completely, over another carton. No water should appear. Would adobe be a good way to build houses in your area? Why or why not?

5. After mixing, spoon the mixture into the milk cartons. Tamp the container so that the mud slides down. The surface of the brick will then be flat for later stacking.

6. Place the containers in the sun to bake and dry. This will take several days depending on the humidity. You may remove the bricks from the molds (cartons) as soon as the mixture sets, in order to reuse the containers.

7. Build a simple adobe construction using mud for your mortar. Plaster it with more mud to form smooth walls. Let it dry thoroughly before using for play.

Want to do more?

Make concrete in the cartons using cement, gravel, and water. The proper proportions for mixing should be listed on your bag of cement. This shows how water mixes with a solid to form another solid.

Ice cubes can be frozen into blocks which can later, on a cold day (Might be fun on a warm day too!), be turned into ice houses.

In each of the block making activities water is the key. The study of the three phases of matter can be related as the matter changes.

You may make a house from each set of construction materials. For the adobe, a wet sponge can be used to smooth the stacked blocks to form a continuous wall. For an ice structure, you will need a day with temperatures around freezing, and a wet sponge or sprayer filled with water to help form a solid structure from ice blocks. Concrete, like bricks, will require a mortar, of concrete in this case to keep things in place. Packing snow into milk containers would provide another building material.

WHERE DO YOU HIDE A DINOSAUR?

Words you can use

length
tall
height
Tyrannosaurus rex
head
jaw
talons
claws
teeth

Things you will need

ball of string
masking tape
chalk
meter stick or ruler

Many children become interested in dinosaurs before they can read. They love to browse through books filled with pictures of these creatures. However, these pictures do little to convey the actual size of these former inhabitants of the earth. Just how big were they? Some were longer than the average house while others were small enough to fit under a bed. This activity uses only one dinosaur for measuring. It can be expanded to include others for comparison if the children are interested in exploring further. We think they will be.

What to do

1. Display a picture of the Tyrannosaurus and talk about it. The name Tyrannosaurus means tyrant lizard. Its fossils have been found in Canada (Alberta), and the U.S. (Montana). It was a meat eater.

2. How big was it? If it were here, do you think it would fit on our school grounds, or in our room at school? In your house?

3. The measurements for the Tyrannosaurus are as follows:

> Length 13 m (43') long
> Weight 6.3 t (7 tons)
> Height 6 m (18.5')
> Teeth 15 cm (6") long
> Talons 20 cm (8") long
> Head 1.2 m (4') long
> Jaws 90 cm (3') long
> Arms 76 cm (30") long

4. Have the children mark each of the above measurements (with exception of weight) on the playground or on a sidewalk using a meter stick or ruler a ball of string, chalk and masking tape. Start from a marked spot, tape the string in place and unwind it. Make a mark with the chalk for each measured meter.

5. The children will easily observe just how gigantic this particular dinosaur was. Tell them that there were others eight times as large (Ultrasaurus 80 tons and 72' long). Is there anywhere you can hide a creature this big?

6. Make simple comparisons — with teeth that long how much toothpaste would he use? How many elephants long is he? How many school buses would it take to weigh 7 tons? How many children could ride on his back? If children lay down head to toe, how many do you need to equal the length of the Tyrannosaurus?

Want to do more?

Do the same activity with other dinosaurs. Compare them to living animals. See the index for other dinosaur activities.

SCIENCE FOR A CROWD:
CIRCLE TIME ACTIVITIES

RAINBOW IN A JAR

Words you can use

patterns
diffusion
mix
blend
rainbow
colors
shapes
currents
experiment
compare

Things you will need

1 gallon glass jar
food coloring
tape or record player

"Rainbow Connection" or similar song on tape or record

water

Although we all need quiet, peaceful times each day, it's often difficult to convince young children that this is a good idea. It helps if they have something to do as they relax. In this activity, they watch colors float through water in beautiful designs and also see primary colors blend to create secondary colors. Peaceful music helps set the mood for calm relaxation.

What to do

1. Fill a gallon glass jar with water and place the jar where the children can observe it from all sides. This works best if the water sits overnight so that the currents from the top can subside. Diffusion will then occur at a slow natural pace.

2. Play the song "Rainbow Connection" or a song of your choice on a tape or record player.

3. Place one drop each of the primary colors (red, yellow, blue) in the jar. Dropping the colors in from a height of three to five centimeters will cause the color streams to go deeper.

4. Observe the colors as they slowly spread through the water, forming interesting shapes and patterns as they blend into the colors of a rainbow. Note: This is not a time for teacher talk. Give the children a chance to reflect quietly as the music plays.

Want to do more?

Experiment with a variety of color mixtures to discover how colors blend to create new colors. Use one jar of quiet water and one freshly filled jar. Compare diffusion patterns. Try hot water or sugar water. Use small jars and let the children do it themselves. Drop the colors in from different heights. What happens when you use tempera paint or ink? Give the children colored scarves and let them move and dance to the music as the colors are moving in the jar.

BAGS OF ENERGY

Words you can use

twist
turn
spin
fastest
released energy
stored energy
heavier
compare
big
little
small
large
middle sized

Things you will need

plastic shopping bags

assorted items to put in the bags, e.g., clothing, toys, any other common objects

Sooner or later kids will learn that batteries are a source of stored energy. There are also other ways that energy can be stored for later use. A swing is stored energy until released. A wind-up toy shows how human energy can be changed into wind-up energy that will work the toy. Another easily obtainable wind-up that stores and uses energy is the plastic bag. In the bag described here, the children give some of their energy to the bag which then uses it for the race.

What to do

1. Obtain 5 plastic shopping bags from a trip to the grocery store.

2. Place something different in each bag, i.e., cans of food, items of clothing, blocks, rocks. Now you are ready for bag spinning championships.

3. Hold the bag of items in one hand and twist it five or six times. (Be sure each bag is wound the same.)

4. After twisting, release one hand and observe the bag as it turns and spins. Which bag unwinds the fastest?

5. Repeat the activity with bags containing fewer items of varied weights. Why do the heavier bags spin faster?

Want to do more?

Increase the number of twists. Does it make a difference in the speed? Try different types of bags from garbage bags to sandwich bags. Lay your different sizes of plastic bags side by side, put similar objects in each. Wind and let spin. Make comparisons—garbage bags to sandwich bags.

THUNK OR DING

Words you can use

big
little
sound
pitch
high
low
loud
soft
dull
sharp
music
percussion.

Things you will need

assorted containers
in plastic or glass
wooden or metal
spoons

Children love to explore the world of sounds. You may notice this in the way they tap their glasses of milk on the table while they wait for dinner. Thunk or ding suggests a way to provide a science learning experience by capitalizing on a moment of natural curiosity.

What to do

1. Go to the refrigerator or cupboard and take out a variety of containers, i.e., catsup bottles, plastic bowls, glass jars and cans.

2. Put the containers on the table in a row.

3. Strike the containers with a spoon, urging the children to listen carefully to the sounds made.

4. Now ask how these sounds can be grouped. What sounds are loud, soft, pretty, not pretty? Which ones thunk or ding?

5. Discuss various ways to order the sounds, e.g., by pitch (high or low) or volume (loud or soft).

Want to do more?

Use different strikers. Use glasses containing different amounts of a variety of materials, e.g., Jell-O before or after it gels, water, sand, etc.

WHAT'S THAT SOUND?

Words you can use

listen
collect
identify

labels for sounds used

Things you will need

tape recorder

various household items that produce sounds

Accurate and precise listening is an important skill all children need to acquire. In order to be successful in school, they need to learn to listen to details and filter out irrelevant sounds. WHAT'S THAT SOUND helps them learn to listen carefully by asking them to both identify and classify familiar sounds. Their involvement in the collecting of the sounds personalizes the experience. Besides, it's fun.

What to do

1. Start in the bathroom. How many things can you find that make sounds. Try water running in the tub, basin, and shower. Are the sounds the same or different? Listen to the sound of the toilet flushing, someone brushing teeth, or pulling a tissue from the box. Turn on the tape recorder and let the children choose the sounds to record.

2. Continue through the rest of the house searching for and recording identifiable sounds. Some possibilities are pots and pans banging, a blender, a sweeper, a garage door, a washer, a car starting, a t.v., a noise producing toy, and voices of familiar people.

3. Randomly play back the recorded sounds for the children to identify by both source and location.

Which sounds are only made in one room? Which sounds can be made in many places? Which sounds are made with help from people? Most people think of sounds as either pleasant or unpleasant. Does everyone agree on which sounds are pleasant to hear?

Want to do more?

Collect sounds from outdoors or other settings. Many libraries have sound effects records which can be used for the same purpose. Classify sounds made by living and nonliving things. See the index for other listening activities.

LIGHTNING & THUNDER, WOW IT'S SCARY

Words you can use

lightning
clap
flash
bolt
thunder
strike
negative
positive
thunderstorm

To the American Indian, lightning was the fiery glance from the eye of the Thunderbird. In Norse mythology, it was the striking of the mighty hammer of Thor. To the Greeks, it was the flaming spear of the king of gods, Zeus. Benjamin Franklin finally used his famous kite experiment to show us the relationship between this awesome event of the skies and an electrical spark. A thunderstorm starts as a white cloud that forms when moisture rises in the atmosphere and is cooled. In some instances when the air is warm and moist, this air moves up into the cold atmosphere very quickly (at 100 mph) and clouds pile up in dense collections. The water drops that are formed as the cloud cools are carried up and down in a roller coaster action that turns them first to mist and back to drops as they fall and rise. In this churning cloud tremendous collections of static electricity are formed. They build up to a point and then produce a giant discharge that may be over a mile long. This is the lightning you and your children see and feel. The ground is also charged with static electricity. You may relate this to dragging your feet across a rug, touching the light switch and feeling the shock. In the

case of lightning, a charge leaves the ground through a high object like a tree or tower and meets the charge in the sky. You see the lightning as it flows back along this path between earth and sky as it seeks to balance the charges. The thunder is the explosion made as the air is expanded along the lightning's path. So lightning and thunder are related and this cause and effect should be studied so that, maybe, some of the fear can be taken out of the thunderstorm.

What to do

1. Before the lightning strikes, introduce the children to static electricity by having them rub a comb or by rubbing their feet on the rug. (CLING TO ME, See page 38.)

2. Go to the window and observe the lightning. Listen to the sound of the thunder. When the lighting flashes and travels in its path, the force of the electricity pushes the air away making a sound that you call thunder. Listen to the thunder. See if you can find the direction from which it is coming.

3. Note that the lightning flashes first, then the thunder can be heard. They are really happening at the same time but sound travels more slowly (600 miles per hour), while light travels 186,000 miles per second and reaches your eyes almost immediately.

4. The difference in travel time can be a way to study thunder and lightning from the safety of your classroom or house. Just watch the lightning when it flashes and begin counting one- thousand-one, one-thousand-two, one-thousand-three. Each count is equal to a second. A count to 5 seconds means that the storm is a mile away. You could also use a stopwatch to time the seconds.

5. Count the wait time for the next flash. If it is less, the storm is moving your way.

Want to do more?

Show movies of lightning. Have a meteorologist come in to talk. Do any activity on static electricity. Read stories from mythology on lightning.

MUSHY, SLUSHY, MELTY SNOW

An awareness of the different forms that water takes is a part of every child's science learning. There is the liquid form we call water; there is the solid, frozen form, ice. The other more difficult to understand form is gas, or water vapor. We also have slush, snow, clouds, hail, and rain that combine or modify water's basic three forms. This activity uses snow, one of those modified forms of water and asks the children to change it from the solid form to the liquid. The more inventive the children are, the more fun they'll have. They may even come up with ways to melt snow that you never thought of trying.

What to do

1. Bring in and have stored in a cold place the baby food jars half full of packed snow. A smaller amount will melt faster, something you may want to consider in planning.

2. Discuss what happens to snow when it is brought inside. Show how water is formed when this material melts in your hands. The heat from your hands causes the snow to melt.

3. Give each child a container with snow and ask them to help the snow to melt. How can they make the jar warmer so the snow melts faster? They can use their hands, breathe on it, put it under their shirts or anything else they can come up with. Just be sure that the lids stay on tight.

4. As the snow melts in containers, discuss what conditions are best for melting snow. Use the terms liquid, melt, cold, and heat, regarding the snow changing to water. One discovery you will make is "the more heat applied, the faster it will melt." Another discovery will be that mixing the snow by shaking occasionally will hurry the melting process. Asking the children to describe how they made their snow melt will help the group discover these facts for themselves.

Want to do more?

Use a thermometer to note temperature changes as the snow heats up and melts. Change the water back into a solid by refreezing it and compare it to the original snow. How many words can you think of to describe snow, ice, and water?

TICKET TO THE MOON

Words you can use

moon
night
full moon
half moon
3/4 moon
crescent
cycle

Things you will need

photos or drawings showing the moon in different stages of its cycle

ticket box
calendar

moon tickets (small papers with a 1/2 dollar size circle on each)

The moon is the most apparent object in the night sky, so familiar that even cows can jump over it! It is also the most easily studied of all celestial bodies particularly during the winter months when it rises before bedtime. A fantasy trip to the moon is the culmination of a few weeks of observing and recording its cycles.

What to do

1. Choose a time of year when the moon is visible early in the evening. It's fun to begin with the new moon and watch it grow. Check a calendar showing moon cycles to help in planning.

2. Show the children pictures of the moon and help them focus on the different shapes of the moon. You can even put them in order from the smaller "fingernail moon" to a full moon. "Did anyone see the moon last night? What shape is it now? Let's find out."

3. Give each of the children a moon ticket to take home with a note for their parents explaining that they are to observe the moon and fill in the circle on the moon ticket to show the moon's shape as they observed it.

4. The next day, look at the returned tickets and draw the moon on the calendar. Put the tickets in a ticket box which the children have decorated with moons and stars. As always, encourage full participation, but don't penalize those who don't return the tickets. All you actually need are a few reports each day. Continue 2 or 3 days a week until the full moon. With luck, clouds won't get in your way. As the cycle progresses talk about the various stages - new moon, half moon, etc, and refer to your pictures. Guess what the moon will look like next? Will it be bigger or smaller?

5. When you reach the full moon, cash in your tickets for an imaginary trip to the moon (see SPACE HELMETS, page 144) or have a Full Moon Party with moon shaped snacks (round or crescent shaped cookies, cheese, or toast) and moon juice (You can think that up yourself!) to drink.

Want to do more?

Share pictures of lunar landings and talk about the space program. NASA has some excellent resources. Read some poems, folk tales and stories about the moon. Sample those from around the world. Write some of your own.

SUNDAY	MONDAY	TUESDAY	WEDNESDAY	THURSDAY	FRIDAY	SATURDAY
				1	2	3
4	5	6	7	8	9	10
11	12	13	14	15	16	17
18	19	20	21	22	23	24
25	26	27	28	29	30	31

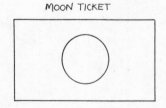

MOON TICKET

WEATHER OR NOT I SHOULD WEAR IT

Dressing up is a play activity that is common in most preschools. It teaches a variety of skills that are necessary for the educational development of any child, such as fine and gross motor coordination, color and number recognition, and size discrimination. The child who chooses clothing is constantly categorizing and classifying. Add the weather unit to this familiar activity, and you bring together a set of skills that teach about the seasons and variations in weather.

Words you can use

seasons, spring, fall, winter, summer
hot, warm, cool, cold
climate
temperature
thermometer
weather
snow
rain
sun
freezing

Things you will need

sun hat
sunglasses
beach towel

warm weather clothing
cool and cold weather clothing

demonstration thermometer (See illustration)

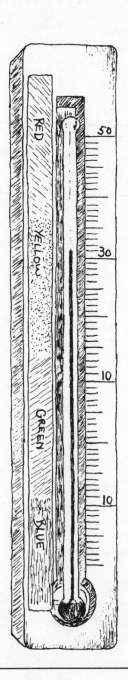

What to do

1. Make a large demonstration thermometer.

2. Color code it as shown in illustration.

3. Let the children bring in clothing that they wear in various seasons.

4. Discuss the weather and seasons that are present in your local area at particular times of the year, i.e. Christmas, Fourth of July, Labor Day, Easter.

5. Have one of the children dressed in a T-Shirt and shorts stand in front of the class as a model to be dressed.

6. Hold up the demonstration thermometer. Let's pretend that it is July 7th. What do you think our thermometer will read? HOT, WARM, COOL, COLD? How do you think our friend's body feels? How should we dress our friend?

7. Have the children imagine a variety of seasons and weather conditions and dress appropriately.

8. Discuss how the weather and seasons influence how they dress.

Want to do more?

Fantasize climates in various parts of the country and/or world using the demonstration thermometer. What do you think children wear in Alaska, Hawaii, Mexico or on the desert? Show pictures or slides of children in various clothing from other countries or climates. Use a real thermometer. See THERMOMETER PLAY, page 101.

WHAT'S THE COLOR OF THE DAY

Words you can use

match
compare
how many
color names
graph

Things you will need

small swatches of material in various colors or paint chips from paint store

easel-sized paper

markers or crayons

assorted colored construction paper cut into 1 inch squares

glue or paste

The world is a mass of colors which makes it a bright, beautiful, and exciting place. WHAT'S THE COLOR OF THE DAY focuses on color concepts through the scientific process of matching and graphing. It's simple to do with the help of colored paper squares or beads that can be turned into a graph even by non-counters.

What to do

1. On Monday pass out swatches of material that are of one color, e.g. blue. You will need to select a color for each day of the week, e.g.,Tuesday might be yellow, Wednesday might be green etc.

2. Ask the children to find in the room as many matches to the color as possible. Findings are recorded by the teacher and a graph is made of all the things that match the color of the day. For example, on blue day a 1 inch blue square of construction paper would be handed out for each blue item found. The graph is formed by drawing a baseline on a large piece of paper. Below the line, write the color word in that color. Paste the 2 centimeter color squares above the line to form the first column of a bar graph. Choose a color each day for several days to complete the graph.

3. At the end of the week, compare the columns. Which color has the most squares? Are there any with none? Which was easiest to find? With some children, you may want to count the squares and compare results that way. Think about what objects you found for each color. How many of them can you remember?

Want to do more?

Let the children predict the number of color matches that they think they will find on a particular day. The same process can be used for matching shapes, textures, or anything else. Look for the same color inside, then outside. Is there a difference in the number you find? When outside, look for the same color at different times of the year and make a record to compare your findings.

ZERO AND COUNTING

Words you can use

zero
magnets
attract
chart

Things you will need

2 or 3 magnets

a collection of objects, several of each — paperclips, pennies, toothpicks, washers, nails, paper squares, etc.

a large sheet of paper

a marker or crayon

All children find magnets fascinating. Their unknown force is like magic. In fact, it is a magic that the scientific world has yet to unravel. Scientists know how a magnet reacts, but can't explain the actual cause of this phenomena. Like real scientists, children love to experiment with magnets. They should have plenty of opportunity to do so before this activity is introduced. Its purpose is not to introduce magnets, but to use them as a motivating tool for working with the concept of zero. Of course, a little science on the side doesn't hurt!

What to do

1. Show the children the magnet which has previously been available for their use in the classroom. Wonder aloud how strong the magnet is and suggest testing it.

2. Bring out your collection of objects. Have a child hold the magnet while you suspend paper clips from it end to end. You will probably be able to suspend two to five depending on the strength of your magnet. Count them together. Make a chart divided into two parts, one side listing (or picturing) the object, the other recording the number the magnet held (see illustration). You can use numbers and then actually draw the correct number of objects. Continue with other groups of objects the magnet attracts, allowing the children to handle the magnet and if possible, record their own findings.

3. After several successes, introduce an object the magnet won't attract, such as a toothpick. Try another magnet. Hmm? Wonder what's going on? Some of the children who have had experience with what magnets will and won't attract may have some answers. Discuss their ideas, but don't declare any hard and fast conclusions yet. Now - how do we record "no toothpicks?" Introduce zero as the numeral that means "none." Continue with the rest of your objects at random, recording the findings. Place the nonattracted objects in one place.

4. In closing, review your chart allowing the children to do the reading. Reread the zero categories emphasizing that zero means none. At this point, you or the children may want to draw some conclusion about what kinds of materials magnets will or will not attract.

Want to do more?

A wide assortment of magnets and objects can be made available for free exploration. If appropriate, children can be encouraged to make their own charts. Have a magnet championship comparing the powers of several magnets. If possible, obtain a sample of magnetite or loadstone from a scientific supply company, museum or high school earth science teacher. Show the children that this natural magnet works the same way.

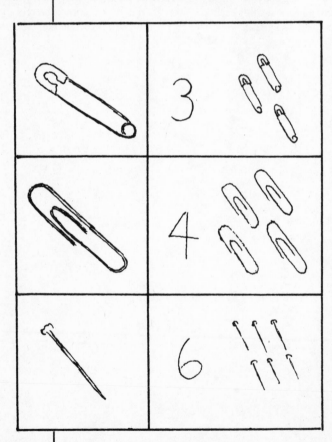

DINO TONGUE TWISTER

Words you can use

dinosaur names
dinosaur
reptile
herbivore
omnivore
carnivore

Things you will need

pictures cards of dinosaurs with the following information on the back of the cards: phonetic spellings of names, pictures of meat or plant or both — whichever the specific dinosaur preferred, meaning of names, length and weight of dinosaur, other information regarding this dinosaur

Although the words that name the dinosaurs are based on the unfamiliar Latin of the scientist, they somehow are easily pronounced by the same child who may mispronounce simple two syllable words. Just as children love to show us what big things they can carry, they love being able to say huge words. The fact that many children are intrigued by the size and appearance of the creatures helps, too. Whatever the reasons, some children learn to identify, name, and describe dinosaurs with ease. By the way, even scientists are not in agreement as to the pronunciation of some dinosaur names. Just do your best!

What to do

1. Show the children one card at a time. Ask them what they would call this dinosaur. Why? Pronounce the actual name. Share what the name means, along with other information on the dinosaur taken from the back of each card.

2. Ask the children to sort the cards into meat eaters and plant eaters. What does this mean? As you look at the pictures can you tell which dinosaurs are plant or meat eaters? Looking at the jaw structure helps. Some animals eat both plants and animals. They are called omnivores. And remember, scientists are only guessing about what dinosaurs ate, just as you are when you look at jaw structures and make your guesses.

Want to do more?

Look at a real fossil. Shells and ferns are especially easy for children to identify. Bring in some of the countless books on dinosaurs for the children to peruse. See the index for other dinosaur activities.

I'VE GOT A HUNCH, SEED

Words you can use

sprout
hypothesis
germinate
size
guess
hunch

Things you will need

seeds of different sizes — large, medium, and small

sealable plastic sandwich bags

paper towels
water

What is an hypothesis? It is a hunch or guess as to what is expected as the result of an action. This activity affords young children the opportunity to develop a hypothesis and to gain understanding of this term by actual experience. "What will happen if I do this?" is something that children should experience repeatedly. With supervision, they can experiment and try things without creating problems for themselves. The following activity should be just one of many such experiences.

What to do

1. Discuss what is meant by developing a hypothesis; that it is what you think will happen as a result of something you do.

2. Pass out small plastic baggies that contain a folded paper towel that has been moistened well. Pour out any excess water so that the seeds won't rot.

3. Place seeds of different sizes in the moistened baggies.

4. Do you think that the size of the seed makes a difference in the time needed for them to sprout or germinate?

5. Form a hypothesis to state what you think will happen. Your hypothesis might be that:
    1. small seeds will germinate first
    2. large seeds will germinate first
    3. they will all germinate at the same time

6. Place the seeds of varying sizes in the baggies, close them, and place them where they can be observed for a week.

7. Which hypothesis was correct?

Want to do more?

Use different types of seeds. Will lettuce seeds germinate before radish, pepper, pumpkin or others? Try experiments introducing other variables such as amount of moisture in the bag, germinating in light or dark, etc. so that the children to try out their hunches.

LET THERE BE LIGHT

Words you can use

fluorescent
incandescent
black light
batteries
flashlight
energy
explore
source

Things you will need

light sources —
candle, flashlight,
electric lights

light bulb cards —
3x5 cards with a
picture of a light
bulb on them.

Each day as we wake up in the morning we open our eyes to light. Where does this light come from? The sun! Are there any other sources of light? What does light do for us? Light plays an important role in the lives of children and their families. This activity explores the phenomenon of light, it's source and uses.

What to do

1. This is a "find a light" walk, and the teacher should make sure that examples will be found that represent a variety of light producing sources such as: the sun, a flashlight, a candle, UV (black) lights, fluorescent lights, and incandescent lights. You may have many sources of incandescent light available such as night lights, lamps, projectors and overhead lights.

2. Show the children the lightbulb cards. Ask them to find light sources in the room or center. When they find a light source, they are to get a lightbulb card and tape it by the light. When no more light sources are found, it's time to discover what makes the various light sources work.

3. With the children, look at one a light type, discussing the energy source that produces the light. For example, what makes a flashlight work? Have a number of flashlights to explore. Take out

the batteries, put them back. Does the light work in every case? Take away the source (batteries) and the light goes out. This is a light source that is a safe model for children to explore.

4. Discuss other sources until all have been explored. In your discussions, focus on both the sources of the light and its uses.

5. Now can the children find light sources they have missed?

Want to do more?

Show the children an ultraviolet light and a candle. Determine which form of light is strongest. Compare the heat given off by the light sources. List the sources of light under categories of electric, burning, battery, and solar. Make a light list for each child's home. Draw a picture of that house, and make a light map of it.

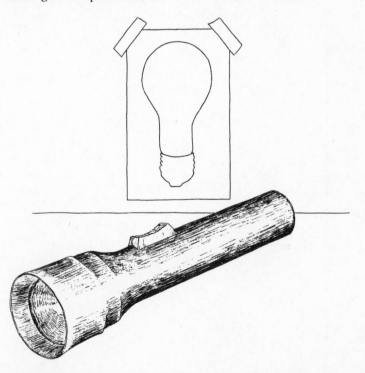

SHADOW, SHADOW ON THE WALL

Words you can use

light
shadow
shape
match
same
different

Things you will need

filmstrip or
overhead projector
or large flashlight

familiar animal
shapes cut from
cardboard or heavy
paper

blocks and
containers that form
traditional three
dimensional shapes

screen (sheet, piece
of white paper, etc.)

Shadow play at its simplest is fun for even very young children. At a more complex level, it can help older children move into abstract thinking and reasoning skills. The basic game in this activity asks children to identify an object by the shadow it casts. It's not easy at first, but it becomes fun, especially when the children realize that the same object can often make many different shadows. Young children can begin with simple and straightforward matching. As they gain experience, the game can become complex enough to trick even the grown ups.

What to do

1. Begin by showing the animal shapes to the children. Be sure that they can identify them.

2. Place a shape in front of the light so that its shadow is projected onto the screen. Can they name the animal? Do this with all the shapes.

3. Place the shape in a different position e.g., upside down. Discuss the differences in the shadow it makes. Have the children move the shape around to discover how many different shapes can be made with the same animal cutout.

4. When all the shapes have been mastered, then play "What's My Name?" Have a child chose one of the blocks or containers and place it in front or the light. The other children can then guess the identity of the shape. To begin with, you may want to have objects in pairs so that those guessing can choose a match by sight rather than from memory.

Want to do more?

Make shadow puppets to use for dramatic play. What kind of shadows do clear objects make? Can the children use several objects to create a shadow collage?

PAINTS AND PRINTS:
SCIENTIFIC ART

COLOR MY PETALS

Words you can use

stem
flower name
flower
blossom
absorb

Things you will need

food coloring
water
glass or jar

white flowers
(Queen Anne's Lace,
mums, etc.)

Late summer each year the road sides and the country are filled with a lovely white flower called Queen Anne's Lace. This relative of the carrot is an excellent subject for an experiment that shows the movement of water through a plant. Traditionally celery is placed in colored water and the results show the colored water ascending through the celery stalk to the top of the stem. This project does the same but the end products are gently colored blossoms instead of red celery.

What to do

1. Choose a white flower. Cut off all but 15 cm (6 in.) of the stem. Cut the stems off at a slant.

2. Mix up a colored water solution by adding ten drops of food coloring to 60 ml (1/4 c) of water.

3. Place this colored mixture in the glass.

4. Place the flower stems in the solution to allow the stem to pull the colored water up into the flower. The blossoms will gradually take on a pastel hue of the color they have drawn up.

5. Have the children observe the solution, watching for an appearance of color in the flower. The teacher should explain that normally a plant has roots that begin the work of transporting water up the stem. Describe the roots of a plant, then the stem, with its function of fluid transportation and support. The leaves serve to make food and the flower produces seeds. All parts need water and get it through the plant's "plumbing" system. This experiment shows that happening.

6. When flowers have been colored, they may be dried, put in an arrangement, or given to the children.

Want to do more?

White mums can be purchased from the flower shop and dyed for Mother's Day. Use celery to see the actual colored mixture rising up through the stem. Try mixing food coloring to change flower color. Start with one primary color and switch to another to dye the flower. If you really want to do lots of dyeing, check with a florist for chemicals that enhance water uptake.

EYE DROPPER ART

Words you can use

eye dropper
color words
air pressure
squeeze
squirt
liquid

Things you will need

tempera paint
white paper
eye droppers
water
small cups
food coloring

The purpose of this exercise is to explore the use of the eye-dropper as both a scientific tool and as an object to be used to create art. The eyedropper itself works because of air pressure. When the child squeezes the bulb end, air is forced out as the space inside the dropper is decreased. The air acting on the surface of the liquid causes material to be pushed up into the tube when the bulb is released. There is some suction occurring as the flexible tube returns to its original shape, but most of the action is caused by air pressure. As children experiment with the droppers, their movements will become more controlled and they will produce some very lovely works of art. The paintings will be especially pretty if you choose harmonizing colors of paint, such as red and yellow, red and blue, or blue and yellow.

What to do

1. Give each child a container of lightly colored water, an eyedropper, and a small container to catch the water.

2. Explain to the children how the dropper works and allow them time to practice using it, and to explore the workings of the liquid-dropper system.

3. Mix fairly runny mixtures of the tempera paints the children will be using.

4. When they have mastered the use of the eyedroppers, give them paper and small containers of the paint.

6. Drops from the dropper will hit the paper and the range of ideas for design will be developed as the children explore.

7. Allow the paint to dry. Discuss ways to use the dropper to change the way the paint is applied.

Want to do more?

Use different mixtures of paint. Place objects in front of the dropper to alter the flow of paint to paper. Make a collection of eye droppers for a minimuseum. The variety of droppers that the children will bring from home is surprising. Discuss the efficiency of some droppers. Which droppers work the best?

RAINBOW RAIN

Words you can use

color words
water
drip
mixture
rainbow

Things you will need

tempera paint — 3 primary colors

large sheets of paper

easels or upright painting boards

large easel paint brushes

Raindrops falling down a window pane on a rainy day are a part of most children's memories. This activity captures the essence of that experience, adding to it the colors of the rainbow we love to see at the end of a shower. As the children work with paint of various colors and thicknesses they learn how colors blend and how liquids flow while creating a permanent portrait of their raindrop memories.

What to do

1. Mix the tempera paints with water so that each of the 3 colors is a different thickness from thin to thick.

2. With paper attached to the vertical easel or paint stand, demonstrate or suggest to the children that they fill a brush with paint and press it hard against the top of the paper to make the paint run down the paper.

3. Talk about which paint travels fastest, thick or thin? What happens when red paint runs into blue? Discuss the colors the "rain" has made.

Want to do more?

Let the children stand over butcher paper. They let the paint drop from the brush and splash where it will. Discuss how drops appear with paint, then use colored water and compare. Splatter paint outdoors following the same procedure, but let the children flick their wrists to splatter paints on various parts of the paper. Obviously, care needs to be taken here to protect clothing and surroundings.

RAINBOW STEW

Words you can use

color names
mix
blend
combine
change
knead

Things you will need

cornstarch
sugar
water
mixing bowl
heat source
duct tape
heavy duty sealable bags
red, yellow, and blue food coloring

Most kids love to play with anything they can squeeze, moosh, or squash. Some, however, are squeamish about getting their hands messy. Sometimes we adults are equally squeamish about having a mess to clean up. Rainbow stew, a squeezable mixture in a sealed bag, allows children to play with color mixing and squoosh as much as they like—all with no mess!

What to do

1. Prepare the following mixture:
   Mix 90 ml (1/3 C) sugar and 250 ml (1 C) cornstarch. Add 1 liter (4 C) cold water. Heat until it begins to thicken, stirring constantly. Cool.

2. Divide the mixture equally into 3 containers, then add food coloring-one color per container- until the mixtures reach the color intensity desired.

3. Add 3 heaping tablespoons full of each color to a heavy duty sealable bag.

4. Seal the bag and tape it closed. Label each bag with a child's name.

5. Have the children knead their bag, mixing the colors into a rainbow stew.

6. Hang the finished rainbow stew on a wire stretched over the window so everyone can enjoy the creations.

Want to do more?

Putting different amounts of colored mixtures in the bag varies the colors created. Heat or cool your mixtures and observe the differences. In time, these mixtures may get moldy, so store them in the refrigerator.

BEAT A LEAF

Words you can use

leaf
vein
stem
pigment
dye
color
chlorophyll
stain

Things you will need

a piece of plywood
or particle board

pushpins

pieces of white sheet
or similar material
(torn into 15 x 15 cm
squares)

leaves collected
from a nearby tree
a small hammer

Collecting pretty fall leaves is probably one of the most common October school activities, second only to cutting out pumpkins. Green leaves are just as important to study, especially with an approach as novel as this one. By covering a leaf with fabric and hammering, children create a clear print of the leaf's structure along with a pretty picture. We strongly recommend that you find a nice outdoor spot for the hammering for the benefit of everyone's ears!

What to do

1. Place the leaf on the board and cover it with a piece of cloth. Use the pushpins to hold the cloth in place.

2. Using the hammer, pound on the leaf so that the color is driven into the sheet.

3. Set the finished leaf print aside to dry.

Want to do more?

If the class has completed a number of leaf prints, sort them into piles of similar kinds. Identify by name and put together a leaf collection. Discuss why some leaves do or do not produce prints. Try flowers and leaves from house and garden plants. Try to wash the leaf prints out. Do a stain removal test by using various detergents or bleaches on material. Discuss natural dyes (WEAVING NATURE'S COLORS, page 83). Create a wall hanging, blankets, or pot holder cover with these leaf beatings. For the truly ambitious, a quilted leaf print is quite lovely. Print several leaves on the same piece of fabric to make a mural. This makes a great holiday gift.

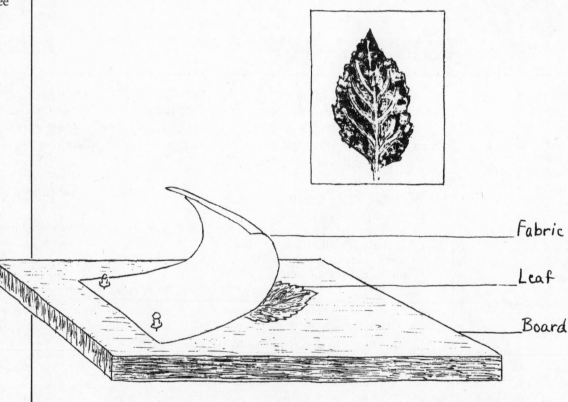

PAPER CHROMATOGRAPHY

Words you can use

chromatography
color words
solution
dissolve
absorb
primary and
secondary colors

Things you will need

water

paper

coffee filter or filter paper

water soluble food colors

baby food jars

Included in this book are a number of activities which work with colors. Many of these have color mixing as their chief objective. This activity focuses on the reverse by taking a dark color, and discovering its components. It uses the science of chromatography which refers to the picture made by colors on paper.

What to do

1. Cut paper strips about 2 cm (1 in) wide from coffee filter. (see drawing)

2. Fill baby food jar half full of water.

3. Place a dot, using a food color mixture of 2 or 3 primary colors, as shown in the illustration. Let it dry.

4. Place the end of the paper in the jar.

5. Watch the water soak into and travel up the paper.

6. As the water climbs the paper, it will dissolve the colors. The colors are then carried up the paper. Those that are lighter are carried up higher. Colors will be left on the paper at varying levels, depending on their density.

7. Remove the paper from the water after the dot has completely dissolved (and it will). Allow the paper to dry and notice the color array. Which is the lightest color? Which is the heaviest? Try it again. Are your results the same?

Want to do more?

Add alcohol or vinegar to the water. Use different colored magic markers to make the color dot. Try different paper to achieve better or worse separation.

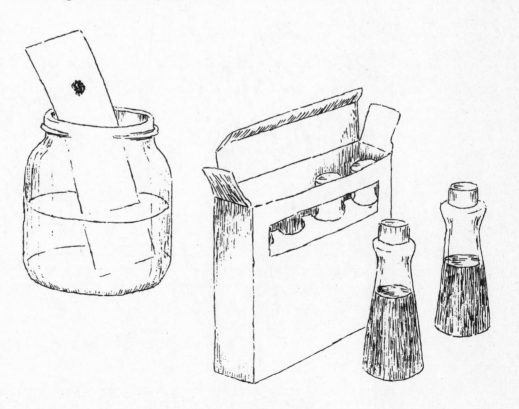

WEATHER ART

Words you can use

pretend
snow
hail
hurricane
breeze
rain
sleet
tornado
storm
wind

Things you will need

tape or record of weather sounds — if not available — the teacher or children can simulate the sounds

paper
crayons

Children have their own interpretation of the world around them. It's fascinating to see how they visually depict the various stimuli that they encounter each day. This activity promotes the use of fantasy to stimulate the children' visions of how they feel various weather conditions might like.

What to do

1. Distribute paper and crayons to the children.

2. Play sounds from a tape or record that depict various weather conditions, or just talk about the conditions that prevail. For example, tell a story about a child who went out in a snowstorm, adding lots of details. The children can help you with this.

3. As sounds are played, let the children create their own pictures of the weather sounds that they hear.

4. Save the pictures, laminate them, and use them for circle time on days that various weather conditions are discussed.

Want to do more?

Repeat the above activity, only let the children create pictures that deal with temperatures or seasons. See "What Makes a Perfect Day" in HUG A TREE. Vary the art materials—use clay, finger paint, etc. Record weather on a chart.

WEAVING NATURE'S COLORS

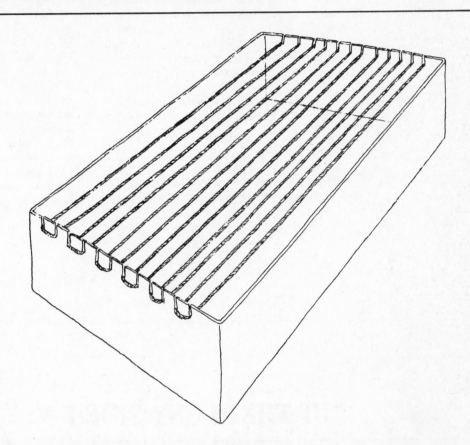

Words you can use

dye
fabric
cloth
weave
solution
stain
over
under
dark color
light color
color names
nature

Things you will need

white cotton cloth (old sheets, etc. — cotton accepts dye much better than synthetics), shallow cardboard boxes, large soup or canning kettles, stove or hot plate

natural substances for dye — your choice of those listed below:

marigold flowers — brown
green sage — pale green
walnut hulls — warm brown
tea — golden tan
spinach — yellow green
yellow onion skin — gold
red onion skin — purple/brown
acorns — tan
berries — pink/red
coffee — brown
dandelion roots — purple

Have you ever watched a child pick a dandelion or a marigold and rub it on the sidewalk, a rock, or wall? What satisfaction is found in making that bright streak of color! They rub green leaves, purple flowers, dirt, whatever they can find. Nature's colors find them as well, appearing on grass stained knees and grubby shirts. Here is how to help them make something more lasting with nature's colors. The ever popular fall nature walk will yield a number of items which create natural dyes. Fabric can then be dyed and woven into a wall hanging to display other treasures from the outdoors.

What to do

1. Place a large kettle of water on the stove and add your dyeing material. You will have to experiment with the amount, the more you add, the darker the color, being the basic rule. Allow the pot to simmer until the water is darker than you want the fabric to be. If you'd like, you may strain the dye before adding the cloth, but it really isn't necessary.

2. Tear cloth into strips 2-5 cm (1-2 in.) wide and a meter (36- 39 in.) or less long. This can be done while the dye is being prepared. Children love this part though some may need help getting their tear started. Strips a half meter long may be better for very young children.

3. Add the cloth to the dye and simmer until it is darker than you would like. When it dries, the color will lighten. Remove the strips from the pot. Rinse them in cold water and have the children help wring them out and hang them up to dry.

4. Over a period of several days, different colors of cloth can be prepared. Be sure to warn the children that the colors will be nature's colors and not as bright as what they are used to seeing.

5. Prepare a loom by cutting slots about 1 cm deep and about 2 to 3 cm apart across each end of the box. Use yarn for the warp threads, running a strand back and forth between the slots (see illus.). When working with a group, it is usually best to make it a shared project with one loom for every four to five children. This allows the children to weave as long as their interest dictates without becoming worn out by "the whole thing". Don't be surprised, however, at finding children as young as four who have the determination and skill to complete an individual weaving. When showing the children how to weave the colored cloth strips, stress the words "over" and "under" Most children are helped by chanting the words as they work.

6. When the weaving is finished, remove it from the box loom carefully and tie the yarn ends together to keep it from coming apart. If you like, they can be tucked into the weaving to make a more finished edge. Natural items such as twigs, dried grasses of flowers, leaves, or whatever you have can be worked into the weaving for an attractive wall hanging.

Want to do more?

Soak the dried fabric in salt water or vinegar water overnight before rinsing to help make it more colorfast. This is not necessary for things that won't be washed. Make a loom for a round weaving by cutting slots around the top of an oatmeal box, crisscrossing yarn, and weaving round and round. Bring in books or pictures about the Navaho weavers. Look at fabrics under a magnifying glass to see how they, too, go over and under. Bring in samples of hand woven cloth to share. Use fruits and vegetables to make dyes. Beets make a lovely pink, though not colorfast. Try commercial dyes. Invite a weaver to do a demonstration for the children. You may be lucky enough to find a person who spins or dyes, as well.

PUT THE SUNNY SIDE UP

Words you can use

sun
fade
shadow
shade
print
bleach
image
match

Things you will need

blue or purple colored construction paper

a flat open space in the direct sunlight

objects to place on the paper to print

The sun is a powerful bleaching agent. It can remove color from paintings, from lawn chairs, from clothing, and many other things as well. In this activity, the bleaching power of the sun is put to work to create pictures. By placing objects on paper, children can see that the sun can only change the color of things it reaches. They also can create their own simple matching game.

What to do

1. Place the objects on the construction paper with the flattest surface down.

2. Place these in the direct sun. During the noon hour when the sun is highest this activity will be most successful. A sunny window will work fine, especially if wind is a problem.

3. Leave the paper out in the direct sun until bleaching (loss of color in paper) has occurred (several hours).

4. Bring the bleached papers back into the classroom. Scramble the items used to form the images on the paper. Have the children match the shape to its image by placing the object on its proper shape.

Want to do more?

Use a variety of blocks of similar size. Especially note their position on the paper to see if changing the position or side of the block changes its image. Use tan grams. Will a hot, white light do the same as the sun? Make a sun picture that the children can use in story telling time. Are there things such as nylon netting, a sieve, or a colander, that you can place on the paper that the sun can pass through? Then what kind of image do you get?

BEANS IN A JAR

A common preschool activity is sorting. Children are asked to sort buttons, shells, nuts, and in this case, beans. What is especially nice about BEANS IN A JAR is that sorting has a purpose. Instead of sorting into muffin tins, the children fill small jars with layers of various types of beans to make attractive designs. They learn even more by duplicating each other's designs. The jars can then be kept or you can pour them out and start again.

What to do

1. Fill a large bowl with the many kinds of beans.

2. Prepare a model jar with layered beans to give the children an idea of what you have in mind. Perhaps they could duplicate the design?

3. Ask the children to create their own bean jar design by filling the baby food jar to the top with layers of different kinds of beans. This will involve lots of sorting as they make layers of one kind of bean then another. When the jar is full, put on the lid.

4. Tape a strip of white paper on the jar and with crayons, color the paper to match the layers.

5. Have the children trade strips and use them to make a jar to match a friend's. Compare the jars. Do they match?

Want to do more?

Use the strips to keep track of all the patterns produced. Do any match? Younger children may need to begin by matching jars directly. They can advance to using the matching strips as they become more skilled. Older children can use rulers to measure the amount of beans used. How accurate are they in duplicating jars with measurements as compared to matching strips? Bring in colored sand to show how it is used to create layered sand art.

FINGERPRINTS: NO TWO ALIKE

There are many features that distinguish one person from another, but one that is truly unique is a person's fingerprint. No fingerprint is exactly like another. Each individual has a special set. In this activity, the children take their own fingerprints and carefully observe the differences by comparing the features that distinguish one fingerprint from the other. The prints are then made even more special by the addition of each child's artistic touches.

What to do

1. Place a child's thumb and/or other fingers on the inked stamp pad.

2. Now press the inked finger on a clean slip of paper with the child's name or picture on it.

3. Clean fingers with rubbing alcohol.

4. Let the children observe their prints with a magnifying glass.

5. Let them compare their finger print with that of someone else. Are they the same or different? What characteristics make them different?

6. Discuss how fingerprints are used to find lost persons. Some of the children may have had prints taken as part of a child safety program. You may want to include this in your discussion.

7. Turn your thumbprints into ladybugs, mice, or any other creatures you can imagine. How many ideas can the children think of? Individuality in art is as important as unique thumb prints.

Want to do more?

Discuss other characteristics that may be used to identify individuals. Repeat above activity using foot prints. Compare to those of adults for size and similarity. Classify prints by their shapes.

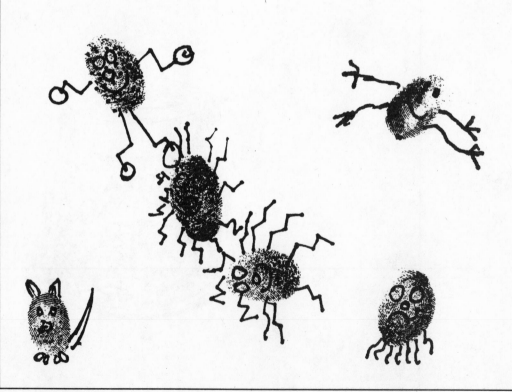

MAGICAL MAGNET MASTERPIECES

4+

Words you can use

magnet
steel
iron
above
below
attract
on top of
under

Things you will need

magnets (one per set up)

cake pan or box lid

paper cut to fit inside pan or box

paint

small objects which are attracted by magnets — paper clips, ball bearings, washers, bobby pins, nails, etc.

Did you ever try painting with a magnet? It seems almost like magic that paint can travel over paper without the touch of a hand. Demonstrating the technique with a bit of drama makes the children feel even wiser when they say that they know it's not really magic. It's fun no matter how you approach it and allows children yet another way to learn more about the properties of magnets.

What to do

1. Place a piece of paper in the pan or lid. Drip several drops of paint on the paper. Put one of the small objects on the paper and paint it by sliding the magnet over the bottom of the container. The rim of the container will help confine the paint and keep the magnet clean. Change objects and/or add another color of paint.

2. While the children are painting, discuss their actions, stressing the position words mentioned above.

3. Ask the children to find other things to use for painting. Are there some things the magnet won't move?

Want to do more?

Use more than one color of paint and create new colors. Coat paper with finger paint and do clean hand finger painting. Use the same set up, but use marbles dipped in paint for painting. Some children may want to try writing with magnets. See index for other activities using magnets.

ROUGH AND SMOOTH

Words you can use

friction
smooth
rough
surface
compare

Things you will need

white chalkboard
chalk

a variety of paper
such as: waxed
paper, plastic term
paper covers,
butcher paper,
typing paper,
aluminum foil,
construction paper,
finger paint paper,
grocery bags,
newspaper, various
other kinds of paper
rough and smooth
objects

Scientifically, friction is one of the forces which acts on objects in motion. It is generally in that context that children learn its effect. As we talk with them about textures and ask them to distinguish between rough and smooth surfaces, there is also the opportunity to explore friction. We can use our fingers to discover differences, but there are also other, more colorful ways. Let's find out how science and art mix.

What to do

1. Distribute chalk to the children. Give each of the children a different kind of paper and ask them to draw a picture.

2. Which surface made drawing easier? Who is having problems drawing? What are the children's ideas of the problems and solutions? Who has the best paper for drawing?

3. Discuss the role of friction.

4. Why do you think certain papers are made with rough surfaces and others with smooth surfaces? Think about finger paints, typing papers.

5. Prepare a set of ten objects with varying degrees of roughness. Some examples are a brick, plexiglass, cans, wooden board, varnished block. These are to be sorted into two piles before experimenting with the chalk. One pile should be easy to mark and the other hard. After the pieces have been sorted, test them for their ability to be marked.

Want to do more?

Discuss advantages as well as disadvantages of frictional surfaces. What would hurt more—falling on a rough surface or on a smooth surface? Many children know from first hand experience that friction can cause painful scrapes when they fall. How can we make an icy sidewalk provide more friction for walkers in the winter? Make a rough and smooth survey of the school. Does the use of different drawing substances make a difference? Look at the process by which wind and rain wear away surfaces and make rough, smooth. That is erosion. Take a rough and smooth walk, but take along chalk to check your guesses.

WET AND MESSY:
SCIENCE FOR A SPECIAL PLACE

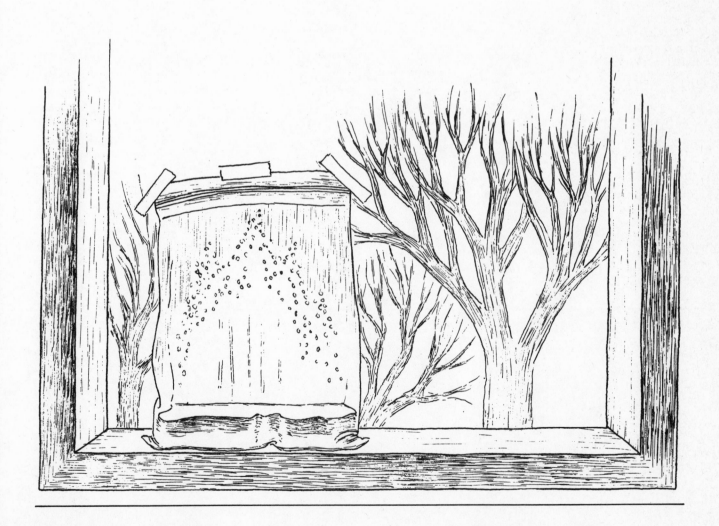

MAGIC MATTER

Words you can use

solid
liquid
gas
change
wet
dry
powder
mix
evaporate
experiment

Things you will need

mixing bowl
spoon
cornstarch
water

Children often see matter change to its different forms of solid, liquid, and gas. They watch snow melt, they see jello solidify, they make clouds with their breath in cold weather. Magic Matter, a cornstarch and water mixture, allows them to compare liquid and solid matter by creating it themselves. Corn starch and water do not mix in the true sense. They form a suspension. When the water dries, the cornstarch returns to its original state. When the suspension is active and new, it does amazing things. It's wonderful to play with, even for grown ups.

What to do

1. Mix water and cornstarch. Hold a bit of the dry cornstarch back in case you have made the mixture too soupy.

2. Test your mixture. It should be wet enough to flow, but dry enough to break off in pieces. You will have to experiment to reach this consistency. The mixture will dry out as the children use it. Adding water will bring it back to the original state.

3. This matter is magic because it can change form from solid to liquid. You can break it and yet it flows. As the children work with the magic matter, talk about the differences between a solid and a liquid.

Want to do more?

Try this activity with flour and watch what happens. Add food coloring and watch the unique way the colors mix. Watch the continued drying process as the mixture is left out overnight. Observe the mixture in a bowl. It acts like a solid. Try jabbing it. Try to imagine swimming in magic matter. Use the index to find related activities on evaporation and water.

THE DUNKING RAISINS

Words you can use

sink
float
gas
acid/base
carbon dioxide/CO_2
reaction
buoyant

Things you will need

baking soda
tall clear container
vinegar
water
raisins

The reaction of an acid (vinegar) and a base (baking soda) is exciting to watch. With a little extra effort, you can produce something even more interesting than foam and bubbles. Carbon dioxide in the form of small bubbles is one by-product of the vinegar-baking soda mix. As these bubbles cling to a raisin in water, they cause it to rise and sink. The effect is a "wow" one for the children. The trick is to encourage their observation so that they see the bubbles form and the raisins doing their dance or dunking because of it. The cause and effect of adding baking soda, the smell of the vinegar and the tiny bubbles form as clues to the puzzle of what makes the DUNKING RAISIN work?

What to do

1. Fill the container with water and add a couple of tablespoons of vinegar. Precise measurements aren't important. Stir well and add two or three raisins.

2. Add a spoonful of baking soda. Don't stir.

3. Watch the raisins rise from the bottom as they collect small bubbles of carbon dioxide (CO_2) on their surfaces.

4. What you are seeing is an acid/base reaction where vinegar and baking soda combine to give off carbon dioxide. The CO_2 forms as a gas that can be seen as it bubbles to the surface. But, some does grab hold of the raisin and when enough has collected on the raisin, it is raised to the surface where the CO_2 escapes into the air. This creates a heavy raisin that sinks only to be brought to the surface again when enough bubbles have collected on its surface. This CO_2 production will continue until the solution is neutralized.

Want to do more?

In place of the vinegar, mix other acids into the solution such as lime, orange, or lemon juice.

DRYING RACE

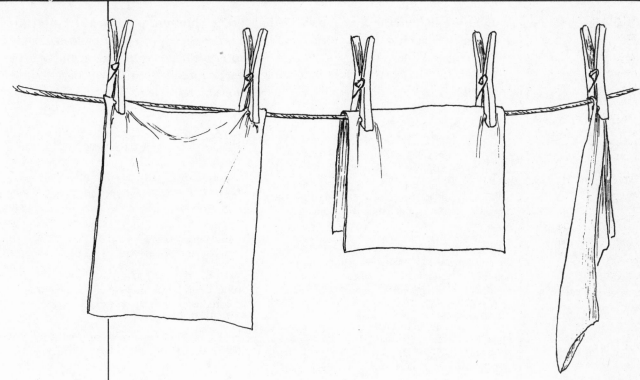

Words you can use

absorb
soak
hang
fold
fastest
dry
evaporate
time
predict

Things you will need

heavy duty paper towels (light weight ones tear)

clothes line
spring-type clothes pins

Evaporation is a regular occurrence in the lives of children. Clothes get wet and dry out. Paintings dry and can be taken home. Glue on a wooden construction dries and is ready for play. The invisible process by which water escapes into the air is rather abstract for young children. They can, however, observe changes which occur. Water evaporates at different rates depending on the material and the size of the surface area exposed to the air. This activity gives children the opportunity to observe and predict as evaporation occurs in the classroom.

What to do

1. Have each child soak two identical paper towels in water.

2. Using the clothes pins, hang all the water soaked towels on a clothes line hung across the classroom.

3. Fold one towel over the line as it is hung.

4. Hang the second paper towel flat.

5. Let the children predict which will dry the fastest. Have them observe the cloths from time to time as the day progresses.

6. When the first item dries ask the children what happened? How long did it take? Why do you think the folded towel is still wet and the unfolded towel dry?

Want to do more?

Repeat above activity outdoors on windy days. Predict and compare drying times to the indoor experiment. Did the towels dry faster or slower? Why? Experiment with a variety of materials and compare evaporation rates.

EGG CARTON RAINBOWS

With very little in the way of mess and materials, children can play with colors over and over. It's much more fun than drill and is quite effective in teaching color names. Mixing colored water with eye droppers develops eye-hand coordination and provides an opportunity to learn color combinations. The children love "making colors" and an adult's informal chatting during the process can help them learn from it.

What to do

1. Give each child an egg carton filled with water. You may want to provide pitchers so they can fill the cartons themselves. With the food coloring, make one compartment red, one yellow, and one blue. The remaining nine should contain clear water.

2. Give each child an eye dropper and encourage the creation of more colors. Directions will prove helpful. For example, "Put a little red in one of the clear ones. Now what color would you like to add? Look at what you made!"

3. Talk with children throughout the activity about their findings. What is their best recipe for green? How do you make the prettiest purple? Can you make a different kind of orange? You may want to write down some of their "secret formulas" and then try to duplicate the results. If this activity is repeated throughout the year, even the very young children will absorb the color names and will remember that they can make green by mixing blue and yellow.

Want to do more?

Use the dropper and colored water to make pictures on white paper towels. Watch the colors separate as the pictures dry. Put the leftover colored water in a jar, add a stalk of celery or a daisy and see how water travels through a plant. Queen Anne's Lace, a summer wildflower, works even better. (See COLOR MY PETALS, page 77)

FLOATERS AND SINKERS

Words you can use

scavenger hunt
find
look
sink
float
search
support
balance

Things you will need

collect pieces of cardboard

wood (bark works well)

blocks
styrofoam
.egg cartons
clay
foil
and other things that can be used as floaters to support small rocks, peas, pins, grass, grapes, etc., and a dishpan or other container for water

An activity that is frequently used in preschool water play is the classic "Does it sink or float?" in which kids test whether a variety of objects sink or float when they are placed in a container of water. Often the objects to be used for this activity are provided by the teacher. We have chosen another approach. Instead of looking for floaters, we are going to search for floaters that can be used to support or carry other objects which would otherwise sink. The children will still be dealing with the concepts of sink and float, but in a little more complex way. Problem solving and creative thinking is what we're after.

What to do

1. Let children collect objects, both indoors and out, which they think may be either floaters or sinkers.

2. Have the children sort the collection into things they think will sink and things that will help the sinkers float.

3. Fill a large container with water at least 3" deep.

4. Have the children place the floaters in the water and test their predictions.

5. Now have them test the sinkers. Do they all sink?

6. Now comes the tricky part. Can they find a floater that will support a sinker? Not everything that floats will keep another object afloat. Balance, weight, and shape are all factors to consider.

7. The collection of objects can now be grouped again. Depending on what you have, you may have sinkers that can't be floated, floaters that can't float anything else, great floaters that float almost anything, floaters that float some things, and any number of other groups.

8. If the materials are made available to the children over a period of time, you will see a definite improvement in their ability to come up with creative solutions to the problem of keeping sinkers afloat. There will probably be ideas even you never thought to try. They may not all work, but that's how learning happens. The children will be comfortable with a few failures here and there if you are.

Want to do more?

Let children "fish" in the water. Attach actual floats to the line and then weights. Observe and discuss how and why these items are used by fisherman. Can you make a floater a sinker or a sinker a floater? Make predictions and then test them. Watch the children's accuracy improve with experience.

 **3+**

I'M FOREVER BLOWING BUBBLES

Words you can use

bubbles
round
solution
liquid

color words

Things you will need

2 liter soda bottles

200 ml (3/4 c.) liquid soap

60 ml (1/4 c.) glycerin(available at drugstores)

water to fill bottle
straws
cups

Want a clean table? This activity guarantees it. But beyond that, it provides an opportunity for exploring color, shape, solutions, and other ideas while having a great time. The learning is limited only by your imagination.

What to do

1. Mix the bubble solution from the above ingredients, having the children help with pouring and measuring. Each child should be given a cup half filled with the solution and a straw. Before beginning, you may want to have young children practice blowing instead of sucking.

2. The children may now begin blowing, allowing the bubbles to fill and overflow the cup.

3. As the children blow, encourage observation, discussion, and experimentation. What shape are the bubbles? What happens where they join? What colors do you see? What happens when you blow hard or gently?

4. Use position words. What happens when you blow with the straw in the solution? Out of the solution? Can you put your straw inside a bubble without popping it? Continue with similar comments, but don't talk so much that you spoil the fun of bubble blowing. It should be relaxed and easy chatting, particularly with the younger children.

Want to do more?

A variety of lead off ideas are evident if the teacher wants to teach position words or prepositions. Put the straw "into" a bubble. Blow and it will become bigger. When the straw is "IN" the bubble you can blow. Pull the straw out of the bubble solution and blow. A single bubble should form. If two people blow, their bubbles will join. How many can you join before they pop? With older children, you may want to vary the temperature of the mixture, the amount of liquid soap or glycerin, use bubble blowing instruments other than straws, or look at bubbles as they enlarge, move, or pop.

LET'S GET SOAKED

A surprising number of young children are familiar with the term "absorb." Let's give them the chance to learn a little more about what it means by doing a real science experiment.

What to do

1. Talk with the children about the word "experiment". It means learning about something by trying out an idea and watching to see what happens. We want to find out what absorbs water. Ask them what happens when you pour water on a towel — it soaks in. What else soaks up or absorbs water? Let's be scientists and find out.

2. Give each child an egg carton and ask him or her to place one item in each compartment. Give each an eye dropper and a container of water. A small medicine bottle works well. You could also use a large container such as a cake pan which is less likely to tip, and could be shared by several children.

3. Have the children use the droppers to put some water on each item. Talk about which things absorb water and which do not. Do some things soak it up better than others? Which things absorb the most

water? The least? None? How can you group the items?

4. End the activity by making two groups — things that absorb water and things that don't.

Want to do more?

Repeat the activity with items the children have collected. Have them predict which will absorb water and which won't. Write down their results, e.g., I guessed the red block would soak up the water, but really only the stick did. Do some things absorb water in other ways — a celery stalk in colored water for instance? Explore evaporation (see page 93). Use colored water to make the absorption more graphic. Some things take a long time to absorb water. Test this by letting some objects soak overnight. How can you tell that they soaked up water? Use the droppers to make tiny puddles on the table. What can you use to clean them up?

PENDULUM: PATTERNS IN THE SAND

Words you can use

pendulum
funnel
swing
length
long
short

Things you will need

string
sand
paint

plastic funnel (Use a funnel that will hold a large amount of sand but has a small exit hole. If the hole is too large, tape a rolled piece of paper over the end to form a smaller hole. This will enable the sand to flow out slowly enough for you to see the effect of the funnel pendulum.)

By the age of three or earlier, most children have handled a pendulum in some form or another. They've played with swings, batted at things hung on strings, or swung themselves back and forth by hanging from a branch or bar. This activity encourages them to play, and to think a little while they're having fun.

What to do

1. Prepare a funnel to hang over the sandbox (see drawing)

2. Fill the funnel with sand and watch it flow out.

3. Have the children experiment with the flow of sand without moving the funnel.

4. Now swing the funnel like a pendulum.

5. The children can explore the pendulum's movement and will soon be able to predict its behavior under most circumstances.

6. Change the length of the string. What happens when the string is long? Short? The sand tracks will tell you.

7. Now in free experimentation, let's see what designs the sand will make. You can vary the force with which you swing the funnel, or make the string long or short. You could even change in midstream. Smooth the sand piles and begin.

8. After the design is made, discuss how the funnel was manipulated to make the various designs.

Want to do more?

Substitute thick paint for sand and paint on long sheets of paper. Put a rock inside the funnel to make it move unevenly.

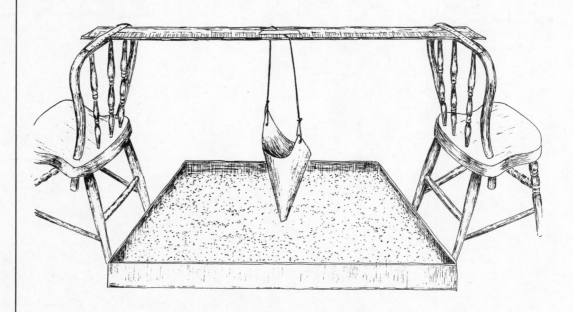

SHINE YOUR PENNIES

Words you can use

acid
salt
corrosion
oxidize
vinegar
experiment
chemical
mix
combine

Things you will need

salt
vinegar
pennies
bowls
water

Children often save pennies and the shiny ones are the most treasured. With the help of two chemicals from the kitchen, salt and vinegar, all their pennies can shine like new. Neither substance alone will remove tarnish, but combined, they work like magic. This is a wonderful activity for those children who love mixing and stirring and experimenting. Think how delighted they'll be with the results!

What to do

1. Prepare 4 bowls with the following chemicals (label each bowl):
    1. vinegar 30 ml
    2. salt 5 ml
    3. salt 5 ml and water 30 ml
    4. salt 5 ml and vinegar 30 ml

2. Add a penny to each bowl.

3. Observe the reaction after 5, 10, 15 minutes.

4. The key to this activity is cause & effect. There are reasons why chemists combine certain chemicals.

Three of the containers do a poor job of penny cleaning, one is super.

5. Now after the cleaning has occurred, talk about what happens, then allow the students to clean their pennies.

Want to do more?

Can other coins or metals be cleaned? Try aluminum (soda can tabs). Does it shine or corrode? Try other mixtures.

GROW A ROCK

Words you can use

solution
liquid
solid
dissolve
crystal
evaporate
stir
saturate
experiment
measure

Things you will need

sugar
cotton string

clear plastic cups or jars — 8 ounce size works well

sticks or straws
water
spoons
masking tape
markers

While we will all agree that candy is hardly the most nutritious part of a child's diet, for the good of science, let's give them a nibble. Growing crystals is a way to teach children about the various forms of matter, how to make a solution, and how to do a "real experiment", with the end result a treat—rock candy. Pure sugar — but at least it has no artificial colorings or flavorings! The experiment can be done as a group activity, but it is more fun for the children if they can each grow their own candy rock. It's really not that much more work.

What to do

1. Fill your clear container about two thirds full with very hot water. (USE EXTREME CAUTION WITH HOT WATER AROUND CHILDREN.) We use hot water as it allows more sugar to dissolve. Add sugar, a spoonful at a time, stirring until each spoonful is dissolved before adding the next. Keep adding sugar, a spoonful at a time, until no matter how much you stir, some sugar remains in the bottom of the cup. This is called a saturated solution. The water is saturated with sugar and will not hold any more. As you are making the solutions, ask the children where they think the sugar is going. What makes it disappear? Anybody have any ideas about how we could get it back? Don't just listen to the children's ideas, explore them. "You think the water makes the sugar disappear? How could we find out if it's really gone? Taste the cooking water. You're right! The sugar's just hiding, it dissolved."

2. Wet the string and tie a piece of it around a stick leaving enough hanging down to reach the bottom of the container (see illus.). Lay the stick across the top of the cup. Tell the children that we are going to get rid of the water so we can have our sugar

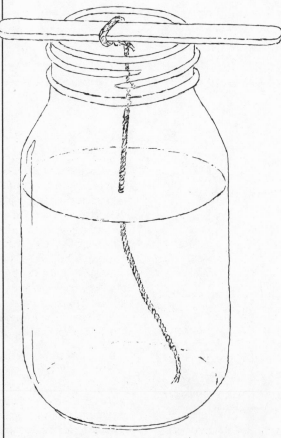

back. What are their ideas on how this can or will happen? Write down some of their ideas, asking questions to help clarify their thoughts. Don't make any judgments. Instead, adopt a "let's watch and see what happens" attitude.

3. Place a piece of masking tape down the side of the cup and make a line to mark the water level. This will allow the children to note the change more easily. Tell the children that it will take many days for the water to go away. Mark the water level every other day or however often there is a noticeable change. It's obviously to your advantage to do this activity in dry weather! If you can place the cups near a radiator or other dry, cozy spot, so much the better. As you note changes, encourage the children's observations. Answers are not the goal. Most children don't really understand them anyway. Instead, stress "careful seeing", writing down descriptive comments. As the water starts to disappear, remind the children of other experiences they've had with evaporation such as clothes or paint drying, or puddles disappearing.

4. When the water is completely evaporated, compare the sugar crystals to table sugar. Break off some small pieces of sugar for the children to eat while you read some of the observations and ideas written about "growing sugar." The rest of the crystals can be sent home to share with family and friends.

Want to do more?

Cover one of the containers. How does that affect evaporation? Allow one to evaporate with no string. Experiment with other solutions — drink powders, salt, etc. Try the children's ideas. Not all substances produce crystals. Not all dissolve. Let them find that out for themselves.

THERMOMETER PLAY

Words you can use

thermometer
hot
cold
warm
cool
rise
fall
degrees
Celsius
Fahrenheit

Things you will need

thermometer
4 similar containers
water
ice
towels

labeled pictures showing something cold, cool, warm, and hot — they can show the four seasons or anything else you choose.

Thermometers are one of the few scientific instruments children can learn to use independently, at least on a very simple level. They begin by learning that the line gets longer when things are hot and shorter when things are cold. With minimal supervision and sturdy thermometers they can do quite a bit of experimenting on their own. They have plenty of time later to learn about all those numbers. In the meantime, let them explore!

What to do

1. Prepare 4 containers with the water temperatures suggested here. Be sure that the water is not hot enough to burn little hands. Place the labeled picture card behind each container.

    Hot (about 40 C or 100 F)
    Warm (about 25 C or 75 F)
    Cool (about 10 C or 50 F)
    Cold (about 0 C or 32 F) Ice floating in
    water

2. Place the thermometer in the cold container and wrap a rubber band around it where it registers the temperature.

3. Change the temperature by placing the thermometer into the hot water. Show the red line going up away from the rubber band.

4. Return the thermometer to the cooler container. It should return to its original position.

5. The conclusion made is that the thermometer's marker changes as the temperature changes. The hotter the temperature the longer the red line on the thermometer.

6. Now its time to experiment. Look at the picture behind the hot water bucket and at the word. Is the thermometer line going to be long or short? Hot or cold? Place the thermometer in the hot water watching what happens to the red line. The children could quickly test the water temperature with their finger. This is hot. Talk about the corresponding picture. Now go to the warm bucket and ask the same questions. The thermometer will drop and the temperature will be less. Move through all the buckets matching and noting the respective temperature and pictures.

Want to do more?

Set up a temperature experiment station at the science table. Measure the temperature in different parts of the classroom. Start looking at the numbers. Chart the temperature daily. Bring in other kinds of thermometers and try them out.

SOAK IT TO ME

Words you can use

soil
seed

percolation
(downward
movement of water)

examine
measure
ground
clay
observe

Things you will need

samples of different types of soil: clay, sandy soil, etc. (a local plant nursery may be able to give you information on various soil types in your area)

clear funnels
water
clear jars
rubber bands
measuring cups

The soil is something more than the base for a play yard. Each soil has characteristics unique to its make up. This activity, in a very simple, yet scientific way, demonstrates that fact. It also shows how soils take in and hold water. Soils are as individual as the children studying them, and the children can easily discover this.

What to do

1. Have children collect samples of soil. Try to include sandy and clay soils. Keep the soils in separate containers.

2. Take two funnels and fasten a piece of cloth over the small end of each.

3. Suspend each funnel over a jar. Measure out equal amounts from each sample of soil, and pour the soil into the funnels.

4. Measure out two amounts of water to approximately equal the amount of soil in each funnel.

5. Pour equal amounts of water into each funnel and observe the water percolate down through the soil.

6. Observe how much water collects in the jar. Which type of soil holds the most water?

Want to do more?

Try this experiment with various soil samples collected from the children's own yards.

FILL IT UP: A QUESTION OF VOLUME

Words you can use

estimate
measure
pour
volume
cups
pour
liters
millimeters
quart
pint
equal

Things you will need

4 half pint cartons
4 pint cartons
2 quart cartons
1 half gallon carton
1 gallon carton
colored plastic

measuring cups
sand

water or dried beans
for measuring

a picture card of
each container —
these can be tracings
or drawings, or the
containers could be
covered with
colored paper and
used with color-
coded cards

several cards
showing equal signs

Children work with volume on a daily basis. They pour juice into cups. They fill containers with sand. They fill boxes with blocks. This activity begins as a free play experience in which children are encouraged to play with containers that have proportional relationships such as measuring cups and milk cartons. It then proceeds to a problem solving activity that enables them to learn more about the concept of volume.

What to do

1. Allow the children a minimum of several days of free play with the materials. They should be comfortable transferring contents from one container to another and know how to keep the sand, water, or beans confined to the proper area. In other words, they should know the rules.

2. Show a small group one of the picture cards and ask them to show you the matching container. Wonder aloud what we might use to exactly fill the container. The children may choose an identical container which is fine. Find a picture card for it and say, "Yes, these two match." Line up the card with the equal sign in between and tell them that the equal sign means "the same as". One carton is the same as the other. If the children choose a larger container, tell them that while it does fill it, there is some leftover. Look for things that won't make it overflow. Encourage them to find combinations of smaller cartons. When they find a combination that works, find the picture cards to match and show them how to line the cards up on each side of the equal sign.

3. Once the children understand the process, they can work independently on combinations you give them or they can try some of their own. Encourage them to predict answers. For example, which containers do they think will fill the quart? The more familiar they become with the materials, the more accurate they will be.

Want to do more?

Reverse the process by presenting several containers and having the children find what they will fill. Cook something with the children that requires accurate measuring. Encourage the children to give each other problems to solve.

RAINCYCLE

Words you can use

water
cycle
evaporate
condense
rain

Things you will need

a large, clear plastic garment bag such as one from a dry cleaners

water
tape
a hot light or the sun

CAUTION: Because of the danger of suffocation, this bag should only be used with direct adult supervision.

The rain cycle is a complex part of all life. It may be easy for adults to visualize columns of air rising to be cooled as the sun moves through the sky, but it is impossible for a young child to make that jump. We can, however, give them a little understanding by making "rain" ourselves. This kind of experience lays the foundation for later, more complete knowledge.

What to do

1. With tape, seal all openings on the plastic bag. Place about 1/2 cup of water in the bottom of the plastic bag. Do this carefully so that the rest of the bag stays dry. Tell the children that this is a pretend puddle that will help us find out where water goes when it leaves real puddles. Gather the bag at the top and hang it in a sunny place (see illustration).

2. Observe that the water is at the bottom of the bag and the top is dry. Now it's time to wait and see what the sun does to puddles.

3. Allow the bag to hang in the sun for several hours. Feel the water at the bottom. Is it warmer? Look at the upper sides of the bag for condensation. Tell the children that clouds are made of little, tiny drops of water like those on the bag.

4. After condensation has occurred, hold a bag of ice against the top of the bag. This should cause additional water to condense. Some water will drip from the top of the bag as the children watch. The cool air high in the sky does the job of the ice and makes rain fall out of the real clouds like we can make "rain" fall from our pretend clouds.

5. Now what happens to the water? You can watch as the whole cycle begins again. Within your plastic bubble you can continue the raincycle for as long as you like. What do the children think will happen to the water if they open the bag? Try it and see.

Want to do more?

Draw pictures of the water cycle. See the index for activities about weather, evaporation, and water.

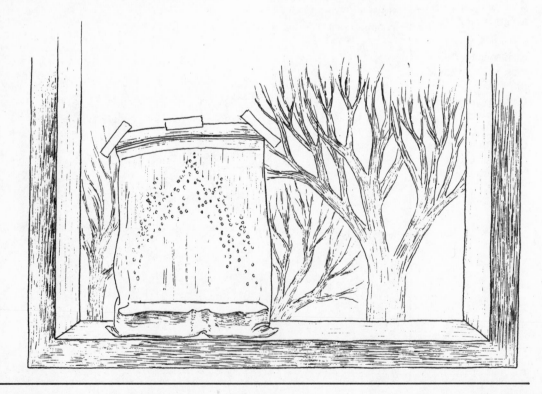

SCIENCE TO GROW ON:
HEALTH AND NUTRITION

BODY GAME

Words you can use

body part names
bones
muscles
skeleton
match
move
roll
shake

Things you will need

2 cubes of cardboard (30 x 30 cm — see illustration) pictures of body parts

An important part of getting ready for academics is good body awareness. Children need frequent practice moving all parts of their bodies in different ways. They also need to be able to identify body parts by name. Much of this comes naturally through play and other activities. Still, it doesn't hurt to reinforce these experiences to be sure that children have the knowledge and skills they need. The body game does this in a way that's fun.

What to do

1. Glue a picture of a part of the body on each side of the cube: head, hand, foot, eye, etc. Print the name of each part on the cube face below the picture.

2. Roll one cube and name the part that lands up.

3. Have the children move that part of their bodies.

4. Throw the cube again, and repeat the activity for each part that lands up.

5. After the children have learned the names of each part on the 2 cubes, throw both cubes. They then have to move or shake two body parts.

6. Add a little music and the class can really move!

Want to do more?

Discuss why some parts shake and others don't. Talk about muscles and bones that control how your body moves. Put up a Halloween skeleton and compare its bones to your own. Feel muscles work as you move arms or legs. Play with partners and touch or match body parts. Use a "Simon Says" model. Move a body part not on the cube. Add right and left to some parts. Think of other ways to move the named part. Can you copy someone else's moves? Smaller cubes can be made for individual or small group play. Cover them with clear contact paper and they'll last a lot longer.

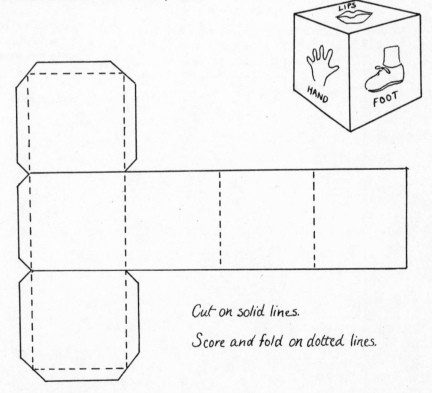

Cut on solid lines.

Score and fold on dotted lines.

GOOD AND JUICY

Words you can use

cut up
add
mix
blend
taste
combinations
suspension
fruit
vegetable

Things you will need

blender
knife
crushed ice
bananas
dates
oranges
strawberries
watermelon
raspberries
pineapple
apples
tangerines
pears
apricots
tomatoes
green peppers
peeled cucumbers
peeled zucchini
drinking glasses

Fruits and vegetables are the most colorful and intriguing of the basic food groups. This activity will expand the children's knowledge and awareness of this food group by introducing them to a broad selection of fruits and vegetables. In using the blender to make flavorful slushes, you are actually creating a suspension. Once the ice has melted, the suspended solids of the vegetable or fruit will settle to the bottom. That's why we give juice a shake before we drink it.

What to do

1. Bring a variety of fruits and vegetables to the class. Discuss and share them, emphasizing that they belong to the fruit and vegetable food group. Separate them and identify the items as fruit or vegetable. Pass the foods around and talk about color, shape, firmness, texture, and smell.

2. Explain that juices come from these foods. What juices are the children acquainted with? You may want to bring in cans as samples for each. How do fruits and vegetables become juices?

3. Have the children wash their hands.

4. Place vegetables and fruits in a pan or tub and have the children wash them.

5. Cut up the ripe fruit and vegetables.

6. Place 1/2 cup fruit in a blender with 1/4 cup crushed or cracked ice. Blend until smooth. Before blending ask the children to predict what they think food items will look like, taste like, and smell like after blending.

7. Pour finished product into juice glasses. Observe colors. Are they different than the original whole food item? Why?

8. Drink the juice and discuss its taste. Experiment with combining fruits, allowing children to make their own choices. Experiment with combining vegetables. Discuss likes and dislikes.

Want to do more?

Why are juices frozen when we buy them at the store? Have a juice party for parents to show one way to provide nutritious snacks for the entire family. Using a juicer will allow you to experiment with solid vegetables such as beets, celery, carrots, and green peppers. Make a vegetable cocktail by juicing a variety of vegetables together. Freeze all the fruits and blend them without ice. What happens? Make fruit salad and vegetable salad. Talk about how fruits and vegetables grow. Show pictures or look at the actual plants. You can freeze some of the blended fruit in ice cube trays or small paper cups to make ice pops.

LITTLE BITTY BUTTER BEATERS

3+

Words you can use

liquid
solid
milk
cream
butter
shake
thicken
separate

whey(the watery liquid left after the butter separates)

Things you will need

heavy or whipping cream — cool whip will not work

small jars with tight fitting lids such as baby food jars

clean marbles

(NOTE: Chilling the jars, marbles, and whipping cream will help the butter to form more quickly.)

Most children have seen liquids become solid, as in making ice or gelatin. Butter making demonstrates this process in yet another way. Agitation, caused by marbles hitting butter fat particles in the cream, causes the fat particles to separate out and to "grab" each other, forming butter. Once the process begins, it starts a chain reaction that continues until all the butter is separated. The colder the mixture, the more definite the separation. Can the children figure out how to recombine the two? It's not quite like turning ice back into water. They also get to listen to the changing sounds the marbles make as the cream thickens into butter.

What to do

1. Help the children fill their jars 1/2 full with whipping cream.

2. Place two clean marbles in each jar and secure the lids.

3. Let the children carefully shake their containers.

4. Have the children listen and observe as the liquid thickens and the shaking sound becomes less sharp. As they continue to shake the containers, butter will form and the sound will again change.

5. Enjoy your butter on crackers, bread, or anything else tasty.

Want to do more?

Put a tablespoon of pudding mix in the jar and fill it 3/4 full with milk. Shake until it thickens and forms pudding.

ORANGE YOU GLAD THEY'RE NOT ALL ALIKE?

Words you can use

color
texture
taste
senses
same
different
fruit
root
vegetable
raw
cooked

Things you will need

orange fruits and vegetables such as oranges, carrots, mango, pumpkin, winter squash, melon, tangerines, orange tomatoes, peaches, apricots, tomato macaroni or noodles

knife

plates

napkins

While it is true that most children love to eat, what they love to eat may be another matter altogether. Tasting small amounts in the interest of science may entice some of those less than eager eaters to try something new. It also gives them some experience with classification and sensory awareness.

What to do

1. Cut the food into small pieces so that each child has a sample of each food. Leave one of each item whole so the children can refer to it. The number of foods you use depends upon the experience of the children as well as availability. With very inexperienced children, you may want to compare only two items. Other children may enjoy working with as many as you can find.

2. Talk about what is the same about all the things on the plate — they're all orange, all little, all food . . . Can you name any of them? Which ones look almost alike? Put the ones that look alike together. Do they smell alike? Do they taste alike? How are they different? Write down some of your findings.

3. Match the samples to the whole foods. Talk about which ones you've tasted and how they have been prepared. Eat the samples. Did they all taste good?

Want to do more?

Repeat with other food combinations. Play mystery food — guess what is on the plate by looking, smelling, or tasting. You may want to use blindfolds. Sort by similar color, texture, taste, shape or whatever else comes to mind. Compare foods cooked and raw. Show the children pictures of the foods growing, or better yet, see them in a garden. Do plants that are similar grow the same way? How many ways can the same food be prepared?

OUCHIE

Words you can use

cut
scrape
abrasion
bandage
healing
injury
treatment
dressing
Band-Aid
antiseptic
blood
scab
skin
heal
observe

Things you will need

magnifying glass for close observation

calendar for keeping track of days from injury to total healing

For many active children a bruise or cut is a weekly occurrence. They are usually anxious to share the news of their injuries with parents, teachers, and friends, but rarely do they see the changes that the wound goes through as it heals. OUCHIE capitalizes on a mishap to teach a bit of first aid and hygiene. In addition, the children can begin to experience time as an integral part of healing.

What to do

1. When a child is injured, encourage him or her to tell how the wound was obtained. Ask how it was treated.

2. Observe the wound over a period of several days to see how, as time passes, it heals and the skin returns to its normal condition.

3. Discuss how the wound is cared for, i.e. washing, bandaging, daily cleaning.

Want to do more?

Discuss surgery and healing. Has anyone had stitches? What about scars? Take pictures of the injury for later comparison.

SPROUTS

What food can be both grown and eaten in your own kitchen? Sprouts can! These seeds, tiny as they are, contain all the elements necessary for life. Sprouting further enhances their nutritional value. Let the children grow sprouts. It's something they can easily do and it gives them an appreciation for gardening, and how things grow. And too, they are often eager to eat something they've helped to create.

Words you can use

sprouts
seeds
gardening
growth
soaking
overnight
rinse
moist
dry
rot
measure
harvest
vitamins
chlorophyll
flavor
light
raw

Things you will need

sprouting seeds — available in many supermarkets and health food stores: Try red clover, lentils, beans, soybeans, fenugreek, whole wheat berries and radish. (Make sure the seeds you use were NOT intended for planting because they may have been treated with poisons. Also do NOT eat potato sprouts as they are toxic.)

wide mouthed pint or quart glass jars

cheesecloth or netting that can be secured to the top of the jar with a rubber band

What to do

1. Place one tablespoon of the seeds of your choice in the jar.

2. Fill the jar half full with lukewarm water.

3. Secure the cheesecloth netting over the mouth of the jar.

4. Allow the seeds to soak overnight.

5. In the morning, leaving the netting intact, drain the water from the jar.

6. Place the jar directly under the tap and allow lukewarm water to fill the jar to the top.

7. Shake the jar with a rotary motion to rinse the seeds, and tip the jar, allowing the water to drain out through the netting. Gently shake out any excess water.

8. Allow the jar to stand inverted, as, for example, in a dish drainer.

9. Repeat the above rinsing procedure twice daily always making sure that the seeds are kept moist, but not standing in water (if allowed to stand in water they will rot). Red clover and fenugreek sprouts are ready when they are 2 to 5 cm long; beans when they are 3 cm long; lentils, peas and radish sprouts when they are 2 cm long and wheatberry sprouts when they are 1 cm long.)

10. We suggest that you sample them raw by mixing them in salads. A simple salad could include bean sprouts, tomato, romaine lettuce, carrots, celery and a light dressing. The radish or fenugreek sprouts will give a zestier, spicy taste.

Want to do more?

Compare the growth of sprouts. Which kinds grow faster? Compare growth under various conditions such as extreme light, extreme dark, high temperature, or low temperature. Discuss light exposure. More sunlight helps to increase the chlorophyll and improve the flavor. Compare the taste of sprouts cooked vs raw. Discuss various ways to prepare sprouts. Divide the sprouts into monocots (single leaf) and dicots (two leafed). Is there a difference in how they grow?

Note: Use sprouts immediately. If you don't refrigerate them and use them within a day or two, they will begin to wilt and brown and lose their nutritional value.

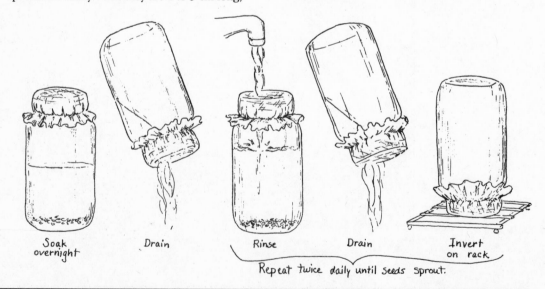

Soak overnight   Drain   Rinse   Drain   Invert on rack

Repeat twice daily until seeds sprout.

KEEP IT COOL

Words you can use

refrigerate
insulate
compare
cold
inside
outside
bottom
top
large
small

Things you will need

1 large and 2 small
cardboard boxes,
preferably with lids
(extra cardboard
can be cut to fit, if
necessary)

newspaper

2 containers of
lemonade or other
food of your choice

aluminum foil

2 closed containers
of ice

We all like to make things that really work and children are no exception. By constructing an insulated box and actually using it, they learn about one way to keep foods cold. They learn a little more by comparing their insulated box to a regular box. Just as important is the satisfaction of making a picnic cooler that works well enough to keep lemonade ice cold all the way to the park.

What to do

1. Put at least 2 cm (1/2 inch) of newspapers in the bottom of the larger box and place one of the smaller boxes inside it. Stuff newspapers between the sides of the two boxes so that the small box is surrounded by newspaper.

2. Line the smaller box with the aluminum foil.

3. Place the lemonade and ice in the small box and cover the box with a lid or piece of cardboard.

4. Add more newspaper and close the lid of the larger box.

5. The other small box will be non-insulated. Place lemonade and ice in it also.

6. Place the boxes side by side in a warm place and wait until snack or lunch time. At least an hour should pass before the boxes are opened. Encourage the children to describe the differences they see. Taste the results!

Want to do more?

Will your box keep things warm? Use strips of denim or rope to make handles for your insulated box. Decorate it. Will things other than newspaper work as insulation? Try other things and compare the results.

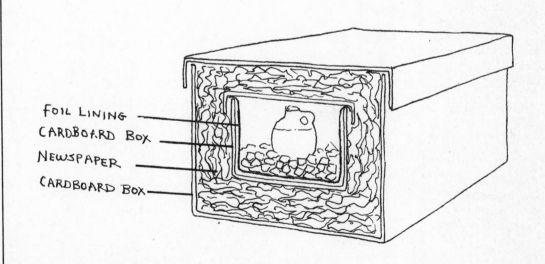

FOIL LINING
CARDBOARD BOX
NEWSPAPER
CARDBOARD BOX

LISTEN TO THE SOUNDS OF THE BODY

Words you can use

stethoscope
swallow
breath
stomach
lungs
brain
throat
cough
listen
think
doctor
nurse
ears
nose

Things you will need

stethoscope
large sheet of paper
and crayons

The sounds of breathing, of laughter, of skin moving against skin, of stomachs growling, and of hearts beating are the sounds of life that children can recognize as characteristics of living things. They can learn about the sources for these sounds of life by taking a sound trip around the body. Some parts will make or have sounds, some won't. Can you hear your brain think? Let's test.

What to do

1. Before the activity starts, have a child lie on a sheet of butcher paper. Trace an outline of the body on the paper.

2. Place marks on the paper at the spots you will want to listen to, for example brain, nose, mouth, throat, heart, chest, stomach, big toe, fingers, hand.

3. Discuss with the children the use of the stethoscope. Talk about sounds made by the body. Caution about being too loud while the stethoscope is in the ears.

4. Have one child or the teacher demonstrate how the drawing and stethoscope are to be used in the science area. Place the materials in the science area and have the children listen to themselves and each other. Can they find noises in every spot marked on the body map?

Want to do more?

Learn the names of places in the body where noise is made. Discuss each noisy spot's function. Have a doctor or a health oriented person visit. Listen to other animals and the sounds they make.

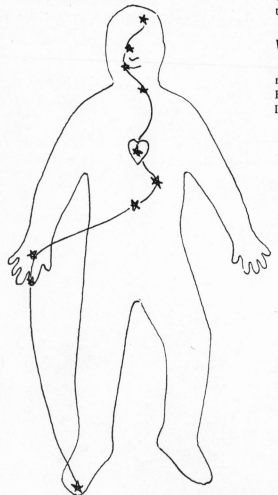

MY, HOW YOU HAVE GROWN!

Words you can use

grow
inches
feet
centimeters
meters
length
height
weight
behavior
appearance
small
large
measuring

Things you will need

pictures of the children from infancy (ideally birth to one year)

a set of clothing items (e.g. an infant's shirt, a toddler's shirt, a preschooler's shirt, an adult's shirt)

ruler or meter stick

a card sent from home by each child's parents noting the child's height, weight, hair and eye color, etc., at birth

We all have a personal identity. It includes our perceptions of how we look, what our skills are, and how much others like and accept us. This activity is designed to help children understand growth and change and to help them recognize that they are important people from the very beginning of their existence. Comparing articles of clothing makes the comparison of baby to child much more concrete.

What to do

1. As a group, have the children share pictures they've brought from home showing them at various stages of growth.

2. The teacher should then lay an adult-size shirt on the floor. Place a 5 year old's shirt on top of it, then a toddler's shirt, and finally a baby's shirt. Discuss the differences which the children can see.

3. The teacher can cut lengths of yarn that correspond to each child's birth length, and tell each child, "This is how long you were when you were born."

4. Have the children measure each other by lying on the floor with their feet against the baseboard — which will be used as a baseline. Using masking tape — affix the yarn to the baseline and unwind until it is the length of the child. Cut the yarn (teacher supervised).

5. Place birth length and current age length yarn side by side. Talk about how much they have grown and changed since they were born. What things can they do now that they couldn't do as babies? It may be fun to do the teacher, too! The yarn pieces can be labeled with tape: child's name, length, and the date. Keep your measurements so that comparisons can be made again later in the year.

Want to do more?

Use a bathroom scale to compare birth weight to present weight. By placing sand in a plastic bag, make a pound weight and a 35 pound weight. Let them try to lift each to get an idea of how much more they weigh now than when they were born. Make a yarn graph comparing the heights of the children in the class. Who was the biggest baby? The smallest? Compare various sizes of clothing from doll clothes to adult clothes? Use shoes, too! Arrange a visit with a real live baby. Can they think of other ways that they've changed?

SING ALONG

4

Words you can use

basic five food groups
containers
names of various foods
names of the basic five food groups:

I   Fruits and Vegetables
II   Meats and Alternates
III Milk and Milk Products
IV   Cereals and Grains
V   Other: Fats, Sugars, etc.

Things you will need

food containers — cardboard boxes decorated with pictures of the various food group

food pictures (check with your local dairy council)

assorted snack items from the five food groups, for example: cheese cubes, meat cubes, fruit and vegetable chunks, and crackers.

The basic purpose of this activity is to teach the children that farmers raise animals and grow crops that serve to fill our need for food. It also teaches sorting and classification using the basic five food groups. The kids get to sing and eat. It's a combination they'll love.

What to do

1. Distribute to the children pictures of various foods in the basic five food groups.

2. Sing the song "Old McDonald Had A Farm" with the various fruits and vegetables, meats, breads, and grains being called into the game. The children stand and then place the food pictures into one of the five food group containers as they sing about the food item.

3. After the song has been sung and the sorting is completed, sit down to enjoy snack time. During snack the children can talk about the food groups to which their snack items belong.

Want to do more?

Add foods to the groups that are considered empty calories or junk food. Kids can sing "and on this farm he didn't grow candy, gum, etc."

BONES BUILDERS: SKELETON CREATORS

Words you can use

skeleton
bones
leg bones
vertebrae
wing bones

Things you will need

construction paper
tape

chicken bones (an adult should prepare a whole chicken to have an entire set of bones)

crayons

human skeleton picture

chicken skeleton picture, if available.

The study of animal bones can offer an avenue into the children's understanding of their own bodies. It's easy to make comparisons if you think of each bone as an object with a job. That job is to support the frame of the animal, to give it shape, and to help it function. By playing with a set of bones, children can begin to associate bones with these functions and see how their own bones are used.

What to do

1. Have children save and bring clean chicken bones from home. Place all the bones in a pan of water and add about 1/4 cup of Clorox. Allow the bones to soak for a day. Rinse them and allow them to dry for a day and they are ready to use.

2. Let the children sort the bones by shape. Can they find similar bones on the picture of the human skeleton? What does the chicken use the bones for? Have them feel their own bones. Compare the way ribs, vertebrae, and leg bones feel. Show them the corresponding chicken bones.

3. Have the children arrange the bones to form their own animals. Tape the bones onto construction paper or cardboard to depict real or imaginary animals. Paint or draw the rest of the creature's body around the bones.

Want to do more?

Press bones into clay or plaster of paris to form an impression. Impressions can be made of single bones or of entire skeletons. Get chicken and other animal pictures and try to visualize the bones below the skin, feathers and fur. Rearrange the bones to fit these animals. Explore with creative movements. How would you move if you had no bones, if you had no joints? What if you had no knees — how would you kick, hop, sit? Try some of the children's "what if's".

ROBOTS HAVE BODIES, TOO

Words you can use

robot
names of body parts
i.e. leg, arm, elbow,
head, foot, ear, eye,
nose, mouth

Things you will need

juice cans
milk cartons
cardboard tubes
tin foil
pipe cleaners
straws
string
paper cups
yarn
glue
paper scraps

Learning to identify the parts of the body is an important part of a child's early development. This is usually taught by touching body parts and saying their names. For a change of pace, help the children make their own robots that will have parts to name. By playing a simple follow the leader game, the children can learn the names and locations of various body parts. The robot makes a routine activity more interesting and exciting.

What to do

1. Help the children make robots that have the same body parts as they do. (see illustration)

2. When the robots are completed, compare the body parts and talk about what they do.

3. Play a simple "follow the robot" game. For example, the teacher touches the robot's head. The children touch their heads and identify the part they are touching as they do so. Their robots could also play this game.

Want to do more?

Teach left and right by teaching children to follow directions i.e., "Touch the robot's right ear." "Touch your right ear." How do various body parts make our lives easier or more pleasant e.g. fingers, eyes, teeth, toes?

SNACK GRAPHING

Words you can use

survey
graph
chart
record
basic
junk food
snacks
diet
habit
compare

Things you will need

crayons

white poster
board — 24"x 36"
covered with clear
contact paper

pictures of snack
foods that fit into the
basic 5 food groups:

I   Fruits and
    Vegetable
II Meats and
    Alternates
III Milk and Milk
    products
IV Cereal and
    Grains
V   Other: Fats,
    Sugars, etc.

Graphing is an important concept that children will learn as they are exposed to beginning math. It is a visual way for children to quantify, compare, and organize. A very concrete way to teach graphing is to relate it to something all children love, food! One of the most effective ways of improving diets is to help children become aware of what they eat. By observing and recording foods that are eaten daily as snacks, we not only learn what the kids are eating but also can make them aware of the basic food groups and thereby reinforce good snacking habits.

What to do

1. Discuss the basic 5 food groups with the children. While discussing the groups, show pictures of foods that belong in each of the basic 5 classifications.

2. Make 5 columns on the poster board. Then draw a line the entire width of the board to provide a box for each food group.

3. Draw or cut out pictures of foods from each of the basic food groups and attach these pictures to the bottom of the graph, one food group for each box.

4. Let the children share what they had for a snack last night. Ask them what food group they feel it belongs in.

6. After determining the food group let the child make an X or his first initial in the appropriate food group box with a crayon.

7. Discuss the completed chart. What do most of us eat for snacks? Create a list of healthy snack ideas, using children's suggestions, if appropriate, to share with parents.

Want to do more?

Have a snack vote game — what's your favorite snack? Which group does it belong in? Which food group got the most votes? Which food group got the least votes? Are any equal or the same? Use pictures of actual snacks to place in the proper food group column.

THE GREAT BRUSH OFF

5

Words you can use

brush
stain
plaque
tartar
remove
teeth
decay
cavity

Things you will need

pieces of white tile (from a ceramics shop or title store)

toothbrushes

substances to stain the tile such as mustard, coffee or grape juice

cups
water
toothpaste

Children are encouraged to brush their teeth regularly because if they don't brush they will have cavities. Did you ever wonder how many preschoolers have any idea of what cavities are? While this activity doesn't answer that question, it can show how food builds up and can be removed by brushing. THE GREAT BRUSH OFF helps increase children's interest in brushing their own teeth by giving them some idea of what brushing actually does. Don't expect children to love brushing every night as a result, but its a good way to start.

What to do

1. Have the children place several tiles on the science table.

2. Stain the tiles by allowing the substances you have gathered to dry on them. Discuss how food particles get stuck in and are trapped on the teeth. The tiles are like teeth.

3. When the stains have dried give each of the children a toothbrush, one for each of the tiles. On some of the toothbrushes put toothpaste, on others use just water. Have a glass of water for each child to use for rinsing brushes.

4. Now have the children brush the stains. Discuss brushing techniques. Brush up and down only.

Then change to brushing side to side. Does this help to clean the tiles?

5. Which worked best to remove the stain, the toothpaste or plain water? What does this tell you about brushing?

Want to do more?

Go through tooth brushing procedures and actually brush teeth. Bring in a tooth and relate the surface of the tile to the tooth's surface. Use disclosure tablets to show the effectiveness of brushing techniques. Visit a dentist's office or check with your area dental association for possible education programs.

LEARNING ABOUT NATURE:
OUTDOOR SCIENCE

ANT E SOCIAL

Words you can use

insect
harvest
prefer
inhibit
path
ant
Arthropod

Things you will need

a plastic or paper plate divided into wedges with a magic marker

a variety of foods, one for each wedge on the plate — moldy leaves, honey, meat, peanut butter, bread, and grass are some possibilities.

Ants, a perfect subject for scientific studies, are found near almost every classroom. During warm weather they are actively searching for food and materials for nesting. Let us see what sorts of foods our ant friends prefer. Caution is advised as some ants have a fierce hot bite that makes working with them a problem. You will not want to encourage ants near your building, so look for a colony away from the structure.

What to do

1. Choose a likely ant colony.

2. Mark off the plate into 6 or 8 parts using a permanent marker. Choose a paper or plastic plate with a flat, low-sided shape so the food will remain separate and the ants can climb in easily.

3. Place small, equal portions of food on the plate— one food in each section. Place the plate in an unobtrusive location so that the food will not be disturbed by birds.

4. Return after several hours to see if the ants have found the larder. Observe which food they are collecting and how much they have taken. Some foods may not have been taken.

5. Note the path which the ants travel while harvesting.

Want to do more?

What do ants eat if we don't feed them? Rank the foods according to which the ants preferred. Lime juice is used in Central America to inhibit ants. Add some to the plate and see if it works. Does the size of the food inhibit ant feeding, e.g. a big piece of bread vs. crumbled bread? Does the surface or structure of the plate make a difference? Count and graph ant movements and numbers. Make an ant movement chart (see index for help).

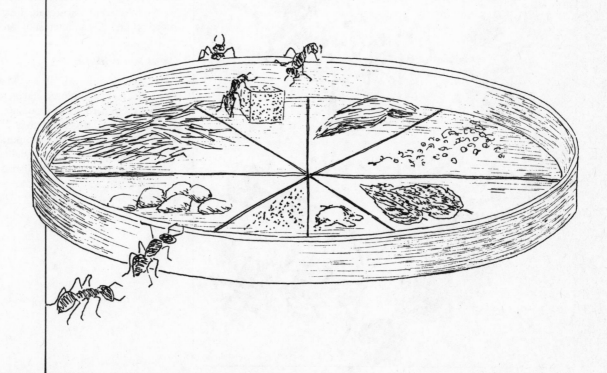

COLLECT A MURAL

High on the list of things to do with leaves in the fall is leaf rubbing. Put a leaf under a piece of paper, rub over it with a crayon and — presto! — a leaf appears. Then the adventurous children want to do rubbings of everything. Sometimes this works, but often lumps poke holes in the paper, rough edges tear, and crayons push through and make rips. By using plain white fabric instead of paper, you can make a whole collection of rubbings without a single mishap. How satisfying!

Words you can use

rub
mural
collection
back and forth
texture
rough
smooth
bumpy

and other descriptive words

Things you will need

pieces of white or pastel fabric such as old sheets

crayons
things to rub

What to do

1. Tear fabric into manageable sized pieces. A good size is roughly 22 x 45 cm (8 x 18 in.). You may want to try several different sizes to see what suits your children.

2. The children can work in pairs or small groups. One or two children have the job of holding the fabric snugly in place while another child does the actual rubbing. They may use the tip or the side of the crayon, whichever they find easiest. The fat, "little kid crayons" are easier for some children to manage. With a little practice, the children will come up with workable systems. Just give them time to figure it out.

3. Encourage the children to move from place to place to find as many things to use for rubbings as possible. This will make a more interesting mural. Anything is worth a try, whether you're working inside or out. You will be surprised at the interesting designs which turn up from the most unlikely sources. Promote adventurous exploration.

4. When the cloth is full, see if the children can remember the sources of the rubbings they have collected. They may want to share them with the class. Give the children the opportunity to make several rubbing murals and you will see that their ability to select interesting materials improves with each new attempt. As a result, the murals become more refined. It's an interesting process to watch.

Want to do more?

Try using a variety of fabrics. What do you like best? Melt assorted colored crayon scraps in muffin tins, let them harden, and you have easy to use rainbow crayons which are great for murals. Compare indoor and outdoor murals. What differences do you see? Stitch individual murals together to make a class wall hanging. Use pushpins to attach fabric to a tree for great bark rubbings. The pin holes are not big enough to hurt the tree.

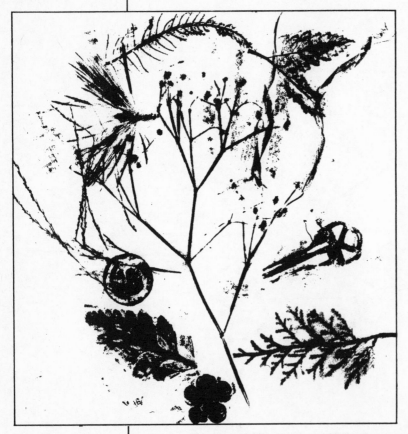

SHIRTS IN THE SUN

Words you can use

heat
light
colors
temperature
thermometer
absorb
reflect

Things you will need

2 shirts, one a dark color and one white

2 sealable plastic bags

2 thermometers

The sun is the source of heat. The purpose of this lesson is to determine which color is the best recipient of that power. In other words, on hot sunny day is it better to wear a white shirt or a navy blue shirt? Let's find out.

What to do

1. Mark the starting temperature on each thermometer with a piece of tape. Fill the plastic bags full of water. Place one thermometer in each bag of water and seal.

2. Place a bag inside each shirt and put them in a sunny spot. Tell the children that we are going to pretend that the bags are our tummies. We want to find out which shirt will keep a tummy the coolest on a hot day.

3. In about an hour, open the shirts and check the thermometers. Is the line still in the same place or has it gotten larger? Which one has the longest line? That means that it is the hottest. Which color would you rather wear on a hot, hot day?

Want to do more?

Fill bags with different colors of water. Which color gets the hottest? Put pieces of colored cardboard on a snow bank. What happens to the snow underneath?

TEENY, TINY TWEEZER TREK

Words you can use

tiny
little
small
hunt
search
collect
magnifier
tweezer
squeeze

Things you will need

magnifiers — one
for every few
children, one per
child is even better

tweezers for each
child or small group

small plastic bags or
cups for collecting

The classic nature walk is a good experience for children whether it is through the woods or around the playground. But like many good experiences, it can lose its pizazz after awhile. A few props like tweezers and magnifiers help children remember that they're outside for a reason and focus their attention on really looking at the world around them.

What to do

1. Before going outside with magnifying glasses, the children need some indoor experience with them. This can occur over a period of several days by having them available in the room for independent use. A basket of interesting objects can be provided for viewing. The children should also be free to explore throughout the room. The care and use of magnifiers can be discussed and reviewed at group time. Very young children will not be particularly successful with focusing the magnifiers, but they don't seem to mind. For them, the value in using them on a walk is that it makes them feel "official" and focuses their attention on observing details.

2. If you feel that your children need it, they can practice using tweezers during free play with an assortment of small objects and containers. This is a highly motivating way to develop the muscles in the hands and is good for those who may need a little extra help in this area.

3. Once the children are familiar with the use of the materials, it is time to head outside. The task is simple. The children may collect anything they find interesting as long as they can pick it up with tweezers. Ask the children to avoid insects and other small creatures that might be hurt. It is absolutely amazing to see the things they manage to pick up. Most of the items are small. However, we have seen a large rock or stick that a determined child has been able to lift. All it takes is one small place to grip. That's real problem solving! As the trek proceeds, talk with the children about what they are finding. Focus on the words listed above and others which will help them pay attention to detail.

4. The amount of time to spend collecting will vary from group to group. Before interest wanes, sit down and look at the collections. This is the time for the magnifiers. They will help the children, even those who can't actually see through them, really look at their finds. Look for bumps, holes, rough spots, and other tiny things. With an enthusiastic adult, the children soon become excited about discovering an unnoticed world.

Want to do more?

Use the magnifier on a walk and just look without collecting. Give each child a tiny plastic cup, such as medicine cups from a hospital. They can only collect things that will fit in the cup.

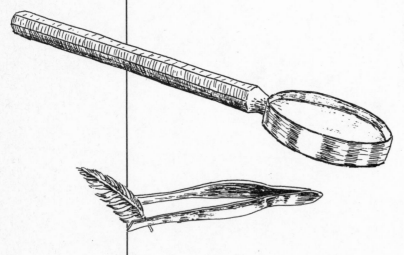

TWIG RACE

Words you can use

twig
leaves
emerge
bud
spring
bud scars

Things you will need

a tree
a twig from this tree
yarn
clippers
knife
jar

The Twig Race utilizes observation of the marvel of spring—the renewed growth of trees as buds and leaves grow from their twigs. But which grows fastest, the twig on the tree or the cut twig that is taken inside? The children observe the growth of the twigs both indoors and out. Who wins the race? Try it and find out!

What to do

1. Very early in spring, before the buds on trees begin to swell, take the children outside to look at a tree. Talk about the lack of leaves and that they will begin to grow as the weather gets warmer and the days get longer. Carefully, cut a small twig from the tree so that the children can observe it more closely. Talk about the bud. Is it furry, smooth, or shiny? What color is it?

2. Tell the children that leaves will grow on a twig that is cut off the tree if it is taken care of properly. Let's see which twig sprouts first, the one the tree takes care of, or the one we take care of. Tie a piece of brightly colored yarn on the twig which you wish to observe outdoors so that you can always find the same one. Take the cut twig inside. Place it in a jar of water by a window.

3. Observe the two twigs until leaves are formed. Which twig wins the race?

Want to do more?

Continue to observe the twigs. Some twigs will sprout roots, others will die. Compare the twigs of pussywillow, forsythia, or flowering trees. Compare them with and without water, and with and without light. Compare different types of trees: which loses its leaves first? Last? In the fall when the leaves drop, count how many are left on the twig.

HOW MANY COLORS ARE GREEN?

Words you can use

green
light
dark
medium
shade
color
pastel
bright
match

Things you will need

large sheet of posterboard or newsprint

crayons in several shades of green

Many schools have color days to help children learn to identify colors. The children wear the special color and may eat foods of that color for snacks. Color day can also go outdoors, and green is an easy one with which to start. What color is green, or more properly, how many colors are green? Take the children outside — anytime but the dead of winter — and find out.

What to do

1. Draw lines to divide the sheet of posterboard into compartments. Use the crayons to color a different shade of green in the center of each section. The number of shades you choose to use will depend upon the skills of your children. Some children may need to begin with two—light and dark green. Others will delight in finding as many gradations as possible. Of course, you may begin simply and expand as the children's needs indicate.

2. The children's job is to find as many green things as possible. As always, remind them of the importance of being gentle with our world. They should only pick a plant if they see others like it. Leaves should be broken off as carefully as possible. All this is difficult for young children, but they are never too young to begin to take care of our world. The idea is to give them a beginning awareness.

3. As the children collect their green things, have them match the items to the colors on the posterboard. The matches will rarely be perfect. The important thing is to encourage each child to choose the color he or she thinks is the closest match. In the event of a disagreement, the collector has the final say unless there is a very clear mistake. As matches are made, talk about the colors using the descriptive words above and any others you

find useful. What descriptions can the children think of?

4. Write a "Green is . . . " poem. Here are some excerpts from one group's efforts: "Green is green like my fuzzy leaf. Green is green like the whole grass yard. Green is green like Jay's worm." Some other patterns to follow are: "Green, green, what is green? Green is . . . ", or "I see a green pine needle. What do you see? I see a green bug. What do you see? I see . . . ". You may not want to follow a pattern at all. Instead, you could write a "green" story or simply write down some of the children's comments. While the writing is not essential, it often serves to bring closure to an activity. It tells the children that what they did was important and provides material to read days or months later.

Want to do more?

Use chalk, markers, or paints to create other color gradations. Choose another color to explore. Count and/or graph the items in each group. Can you find more color variations inside or outside? Is this the same for all colors? How many colors can you find? Can you match each color in a box of 16 crayons? Move on to the bigger boxes. Are there some colors you can't find anywhere in nature? During what time of year can you find the most colors?

LEAF CATCHERS

Words you can use

leaf
fall
autumn
collect
count
most
more
least
compare
graph
guess
fewer

Things you will need

2 large leaf catchers, for example, wastebaskets, bushel baskets, boxes, or bed sheets, label one red and one blue

shelf paper or adding machine tape

The warmth of the sun, the colors, and the leaves falling are all part of the wonders of autumn. It is the time that trees go into the dormant state in which they spend the winter. The leaves have done their work of catching sunlight and turning it into food so that the tree may grow and reproduce. As it prepares for its winter rest, the leaves die. The green leaves change to red, gold, and brown, and drop to the ground. Some trees shed their leaves slowly, others drop their leaves overnight. Some keep their leaves until spring when they are pushed off by newly opening leaf buds. To take advantage of this yearly happening in a more organized way, we suggest you try to catch some leaves and graph the results.

What to do

1. Choose a day when the leaves are falling and take the children outside to watch. Talk about the fact that most trees lose their leaves each fall, but not all at the same time. Look at the trees in your area. Which ones are losing leaves now?

2. Show the children your leaf catchers. Ask them to look around and decide where to put one leaf catcher so that it will catch the most leaves possible. Encourage them to explain their choices. For example, "Put it by the fence cause there's piles and piles of lots of leaves" or "Put it by the maple tree. It has a million, jillion leaves." Arrive at a choice and place the leaf catcher. Now find a spot where you will catch the fewest leaves and put the other leaf catcher there. Just be sure that the opening of the leaf catcher is uncovered so that it has at least a sporting chance to catch a few leaves. Often children choose a spot far from the tree for this catcher, but with the right breeze, it may collect more than the other container!

3. Leave the catcher outside long enough to collect several leaves, at least an hour, preferably longer.

At the end of your time bring them inside and compare. Which leaf catcher collected the most? The least? Were your guesses right? Let's make a graph to find out.

4. To graph your leaves, use a roll of shelf paper with a line down the middle or 2 strips of adding machine tape. Label one side "Red Leaf Catcher" and the other "Blue Leaf Catcher". Mark off boxes so that one leaf will fit in each. Those of you with sycamore leaves will need bigger boxes than those with dogwood. The boxes keep the leaves placed at equal distances just like squares in graph paper. (see illustration) Tape one leaf in each box, first those from one catcher, then those from the other. With the leaves lined up in a "bar graph" it's easy to see your results, with or without counting.

Want to do more?

Graph leaves according to type. Which tree is producing the most fallen leaves right now? Will the same tree win next week? How many colors can your leaf catchers catch? Do more leaves fall during the day or over night? How could you find out?

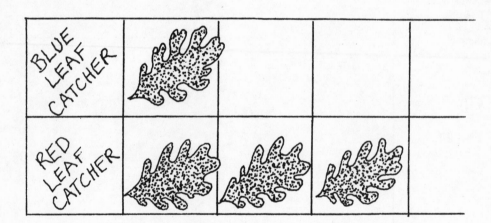

OUTDOOR HUNT AND FIND

Words you can use

any words that explain or define the objects of your hunt scavenger hunt

Things you will need

bags

hunt lists (see suggested examples)

We often take our children on walks outdoors, and we can introduce a creative element to these walks through an outdoor scavenger hunt. The children scour the yard for the objects on their list, picking and choosing to select those that are deemed most appropriate. As this selection process is going on, a constant dialogue between children and teachers can occur with the evaluation of objects being an ongoing, exciting process.

What to do

1. Choose your hunt from the hunt lists suggested based on what is appropriate for your children. Or, make lists of your own.

2. Discuss the focus of the hunt with the children, reviewing the particular vocabulary for the hunt you have chosen. For example, if you will be doing a texture hunt, talk about rough, bumpy, smooth, hard, soft, etc.

3. Turn the children loose to search the school yard or path for appropriate items. When they find objects they are to bring them to you.

4. In some areas, picking live things such as leaves and flowers is not appropriate and may be illegal. If that is the case, then before the search begins a discussion about flowers and leaves and how living things should be cared for and protected is in order. In that case you may visit the site, note the object, and record it's presence on your sheet.

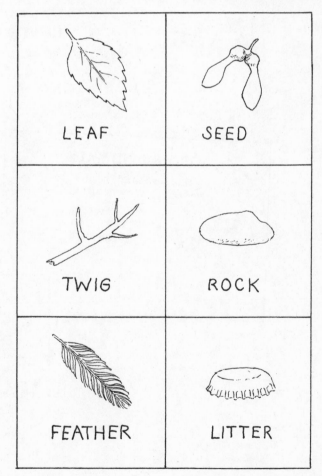

5. You may use one hunt with all the children, or groups of children may do different hunts. Ability to accomplish the task would be the criteria. If you decide to have different groups working on different hunt lists, you may need to have an adult accompany each group.

6. Upon finishing the hunt, bring the objects back and share what you have found.

Suggested Hunt Lists for Outdoor Hunt and Find Walk

Want to do more?

Classify the objects using criteria suggested by the children. Create collages from the various finds. Add to these as you go through the year. Place your finds in a minimuseum.

HUNT & FIND WALK
Your Assignment: Lengths
Find an object that is:

1. one hand across
2. one foot (yours) long
3. waist high
4. group size
5. able to fit in your hand (10)
6. further than anyone can throw
7. smaller than a finger nail
8. tiniest
9. biggest
10. oldest

HUNT & FIND WALK
Your Assignment: Textures
Find objects that are:

1. rough
2. smooth
3. hard
4. soft
5. sharp
6. bumpy
7. ridged or grooved
8. uneven
9. geometric
10. symmetrical

HUNT & FIND WALK
Your Assignment: Number sets

Find objects or groupings (sets) with values = from 1–10.

HUNT & FIND WALK
Your Assignment: Shapes
Find objects that generally are:

1. circular
2. triangular
3. square
4. rectangular
5. heart shaped
6. star shaped
7. spherical
8. cylindrical

HUNT & FIND WALK
Your Assignment:
Find these specific things:

1. snail shell
2. vine
3. a bad smell
4. a great smell
5. a flower
6. a root
7. water
8. over 100 years old
9. will hold things
10. new life
11. something useful
12. something beautiful
13. something you have never seen before

PUDDLE WALK

Words you can use

evaporation
puddles
measure
depth
circumference
rain
diameter
record

Things you will need

meter stick or yardstick,

paper and crayons for recording purposes

Every rain storm brings a challenge of puddles to walk around as the rain water collects in low places. But tomorrow the puddle may be gone or remembered only by a dried ring of dirt. This lesson proposes to use the puddle as a teaching tool to help children predict the possible presence of a future puddle. It also checks the "puddleability" of the area so that the next time it rains, the class can take a "puddle walk" to see if puddles form.

What to do

1. After a rain storm take a puddle walk. Ask the children to see how many puddles they can find.

2. Record the characteristics of the puddles.
   a. Circumference — How big around are they?
   b. Depth — How deep are they? (Use a measuring stick)
   c. Diameter — To measure the puddle's diameter walk through it, lay a stick across it, or stretch string across it.
   d. Where do puddles usually form?

3. Return to observe the puddles the next day. What changes are there from the characteristics recorded on the first day? Repeat step 2. Are the puddles bigger or smaller? What do you think causes some puddles to last longer than others?

Want to do more?

Predict where puddles will be formed before the next rainstorm. Fill a 2 liter soda bottle with water so you start with equal amounts of H_2O. Let the children make their own puddles. Then predict which will evaporate first, which will last the longest, and which will be deepest.

YOUR OWN ANIMAL BOOK

No matter where you teach, from the heart of the inner city to the rural areas of the West, animals can be found on or near the school ground. Students see them fleetingly or know of their existence. This activity proposes to have you and the children develop a school animal guide so that you can more completely explore your own world of animals, and becomes an ongoing activity as seasons change and new animals come and go.

Words you can use

migrate
animal names
season names
adult
young
nest

Things you will need

Animal pictures and magazines

a scrap book
animal field guides
binoculars

collecting jars
and nets are nice
additions for more
in depth study.

You can write to
your state
Department of
Conservation, The
Audubon Society, or
The National
Wildlife Federation
for pictures and
information on
different species of
animals.

What to do

1. Plan a field trip to observe animals in the school yard.

2. Once observed, the teacher should make a definite identification of the critter with the help of the children. Observe and discuss the obvious characteristics such as type of animal, color, and size. Find it in the appropriate field guide, again with their help. You may have children who can readily identify some creatures. Your response might then be, "Hey, I bet you're right. Let's look it up and see what our book can tell us about it."

3. It is now time to make a book page for your find. This page should include a photo or accurate drawing so the children will be able to use it for future identification. It might also include "field sketches" by the children (see FISH—UP CLOSE AND PERSONAL, page 32, for observation and drawing help). Once a picture page has been made, the children can add materials that might come from the animal such as feathers or fur, written information on their own observations, or snapshots. The page should be as personalized as possible so that it is a real reflection of the children's experience.

4. Remember this is an ongoing project. New animals come and go and the key to this activity is that it is never done. This encourages you and your children to always be looking for new visitors to the school, whether they be ants, snails, bluebirds, or butterflies, and adding to your own animal book.

Want to do More?

Collect an animal and keep it in the classroom to observe it for a longer time; insects, small rodents, reptiles, and fish are easily kept. Select an animal of the month. Try to find the state animal, insect, bird, etc. and observe them. Tape record the sounds of your critter. Discuss what the animals eat. Where do you find most critters, indoors or out-of-doors? Make a similar book for plants. If your setting is like most, a field guide to common weeds will be a big help.

This is the Cardinal. His nest is in that tree.

RAIN MEASURES

Most of us have no idea how much rain falls during a storm. We all know that an inch of rain means a heavy rain storm, but what it really means is that every surface that the storm hit received one inch of rain. It would be like putting a one inch thick carpet of rain over everything! By making collecting jars and having the children actually measure the water collected, they can begin to understand just how great the amounts of water that fall from the sky can be. You'll all be surprised!

Words you can use

measure
rainfall
inches
evaporate
more
less
compare
meteorologist

Things you will need

assorted containers children have brought from home such as cake pans, cottage cheese cartons, soup cans, plastic cups, and jars, (should be flat sided and flat bottomed)

food coloring
ruler

What to do

1. Since rainfall is often a surprise event, it is a good idea to have the children bring in containers and store them in a box to "save for a rainy day". This will allow you to take advantage of the next rainfall.

2. Talk with the children about the job meteorologists have. In addition to telling us what the weather is likely to be, they also tell about the weather we have had. They write it down so they can remember it. We can do the same thing.

3. When rain seems likely, take the children outside and place the containers in open places around the schoolyard. Some of them may need to be wedged or weighted so that they don't blow away. Place a drop or two of food coloring in each. This makes it easier for the children to see the water level later.

You may want to put out some without coloring, so that they can see that rain really is water. (It won't matter if the coloring dries before it rains. It will still work.)

4. After the rain, go to each container to measure the water level. Place the ruler straight in and note the depth. Make a list: Shana's cup — 1/2 inch, Richie's pan — 1/2 inch and so on. Write a summary statement at the end such as, "It rained really hard. Everybody's containers had 1/2 inch of water except Paul's because his was under a tree." Date your record just as a meteorologist would.

5. Pour all your samples together. How much water did you collect? Use the water for an evaporation experiment (page 93) or for COLOR MY PETALS, page 77.

Want to do more?

Make a rain gauge with a tall thin jar such as an olive jar. Fasten a thin strip of masking tape along the side of the narrow jar. Fill a wide jar with water to a height of exactly one inch. Pour the water from the wide jar into the narrow jar. Place a mark on the masking tape on the narrow jar that is level with the top of the water. This is the equivalent of one inch of rainfall. In a like way, mark the place on the narrow jar for higher amounts of rainfall. Use the calibrated jar to measure your samples. Make a bar graph to compare amounts of rain from one time to the next. Collect water from a faucet drip. As with rain, you will be surprised at the amount that collects in just one day. See the index for other weather activities.

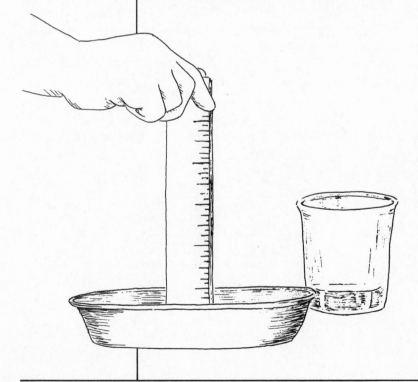

WARBLE, CHEEP OR TWEET: NAME THAT TUNE

Words you can use

listen
sound
sing
bird call
names of birds

Things you will need

Audubon record for bird calls — available free in most public libraries

the Audubon Bird Guide (photographs)

the Peterson Guide (drawings)

a record player

Audubon would have been proud of you leading your charges on a safari to discover feathered friends. Because too many bird sounds may confuse your children, the sound of a bird most common to your area should be the quarry of this hunt. If you have taped the bird's sounds, found a picture in the bird book, and noted the most common places to find your chosen bird, then a search around the school yard should produce it. The focus of this lesson is on the bird's sound. If you discuss birding with real experts, they will tell you that most frequently a bird is heard before it is seen. So with cheeps and tweets in mind, have a bird walk with your class, and practice a little auditory memory and discrimination, too.

What to do

1. Show the children pictures of birds that are common to your geographical area.

2. Listen to common bird calls (cardinal, chickadee, bob white, pigeon — those that are abundant in your area). Play the recording over and over, letting the children discriminate between the different calls by listening carefully and then identifying the appropriate bird. Sometimes a phrase or word can imitate the bird call as in the "peter-peter" of the titmouse or the chickadee-dee-dee of guess who? These phrases are often listed in the bird guides and make remembering much easier.

3. The teacher should go on the walk alone initially. Listen and identify the birds commonly heard in your area. If pigeons are the only birds around your school, that's what you want the children to listen for.

4. A walk with the children is next. Before this walk choose one or two bird calls that everyone will listen for. Take a picture of these birds on the walk with you. Encourage the children to walk quietly and listen for the bird calls. Let them know that it sometimes takes more than one walk to find a bird. However, careful planning should increase the probability of success.

5. Conclude your birding experience in the manner of your choice. Some groups enjoy coming back and drawing pictures or dictating stories about the birds. If you like, these can be the start of individual or group bird books.

Want to do more?

List all the bird calls you hear and keep an ongoing record. Collect bird calls of your area on a tape recorder. See " Your Own Animal Book" on page 134 as a related activity. HUG A TREE has numerous bird activities.

ACTING OUT SCIENCE IN A BIG WAY: CREATIVITY AND MOVEMENT

DANCE A GARDEN

How about a new approach to an oldie but goodie? Creative movement and guided imagery are recognized methods for introducing or reviewing concepts — lots of us remember pretending to grow from acorns to oak trees in our early years. By using a bit of fruit as the initial food source, a plant mister to make it rain, and the light switch to turn on the "sun", anyone can start a whole grove of oak trees, or a bean patch, or a daisy field. The children also get the chance to roll their tongues around the word photosynthesis, a word they like just as well as brontosaurus.

Words you can use

seeds
plant
grow
nutrients
shape
slow motion
photosynthesis
rain
sun

Things you will need

record or tape player

quiet music "to grow by" (for example — "Sunshine on My Shoulders" or Beethoven's Pastoral Symphony)

plant mister with water

an assortment of seeds

enough fruit for each child to have a small piece (seedless grapes are easy).

What to do

1. Show the children the collection of seeds and talk about how they grow into plants. Did anyone ever plant a garden? What do seeds need to grow? (Water and warmth to sprout, sunlight to continue to grow.) Tell them that all seeds, no matter what size or shape, have a little bit of food inside them to help the plant start to grow. Once the plant is in the sunlight it can make most of its own food through photosynthesis. You may want to chant the word with the children a few times. Most of them will enjoy trying such a long word, especially said rhythmically.

2. Ask the children to become seeds, forming the tiniest body shapes they can create. What kind of seed are you? What plant will you become?

3. Turn off the lights. The seeds are under the ground in the dark. Start the music. Tell the children that they will begin to grow in slow motion when they have food and water.

4. Give each child a piece of fruit, but tell them they can't begin to eat until it rains. Using the plant mister, create rain for each child. They can then begin to sprout and eat the food stored in the seed. Encourage them to grow "in slow motion" just a little bit at a time.

5. Turn on the lights. Now the seedlings don't need their stored food anymore. They soak up the sunlight and make their own food through photosynthesis. Oh, but they're looking a little droopy. They can't make their own water. How about a little more rain?

6. When the "plants" are grown, ask them what they are. Discuss what would happen with no rain or sunlight.

7. Discuss what people need to grow.

Want to do more?

Grow seeds with and without water. Try peas, mung beans, radishes, or alfalfa for quick growth. Expose some to light and cover others. What happens? Discuss the importance of soil as a source of water and nutrients. Grow seeds with and without soil.

DINO BODY MATCH!

Words you can use

knee
shoulders
buttocks
chest
ankle
stomach
head
neck
tail
leg
arms
mouth
eyes
dinosaur
body parts

Things you will need

pictures of a
dinosaur which
show appropriate
body parts

In the scientific study of comparative anatomy, researchers compare various animal structures using them to classify the animals. This activity uses an animal that's different, but which captures the children's imagination, to compare and thus teach various body parts.

What to do

1. Show the children a picture of a dinosaur.

2. Point to and identify the following body parts of the dinosaur: head, back, legs, arms, shoulders, feet, knee, tail, chest, neck, mouth, eyes.

3. Now let the children identify and match similar parts on their own bodies, i.e., touch the dinosaurs knee, now touch your knee.

Want to do more?

Follow the above procedure, using pictures of other animals such as farm and zoo animals. Explain that the dinosaur is a lizard and point out some ways in which his body is different from a human body, e.g., scales instead of skin, claws instead of fingernails.

LEAF HUNT RELAY

Words you can use

leaf
similar
compound
simple
rough
smooth
edge

Things you will need

one pair of leaves per child—you should use at least 3 different kinds of leaves (As children become more skilled, increase the variety.)

Recognizing that leaves can be matched is the first step toward realizing that a tree has leaves of a predictable kind and that they may be the same as or different from the leaves on another tree. The LEAF HUNT RELAY teaches the children to look for key characteristics which will help them find a match more quickly. The relay race adds pizazz to the matching activity. It's up to the adult to set a pace which creates challenge without frustration. Timing the whole group and then trying to beat that time adds the competitive edge without winners and losers.

What to do

1. Place one set of leaves at one end of the play area and a matching set at the other end.

2. Have the children gather around one set of the leaves. Talk about the characteristics of each leaf, discussing the attributes that make each leaf different. Allow the children time to explore the leaves and make distinctions.

3. Now the group will have a race. The goal is to match a leaf from this set with one from the set at the other end of the room.

4. At the GO signal have a child take a leaf and walk quickly to the other end, find its match and return to the start. In order to give everyone a turn, you may want to have 2 or more children go at the same time.

5. As the child places the matched leaves on the table, the next child goes until all have found a match.

6. If mistakes are made during the relay, discuss these and where the similarities and differences exist in the mismatched leaves.

7. Practice makes perfect. The children will need time to learn how both the matching and the relay work.

Want to do more?

Increase the number and variety of leaves. Have the children remember which leaf they need to match rather than carry their leaf to the second pile. Develop a leaf lotto game.

SENSITIVE TOES

Words you can use

texture
rough
smooth
soft
hard
slick
cold
warm
other descriptive
words

Things you will need

a variety of texture squares made from rug samples, door mats, linoleum, ceiling tile, wood, bricks, pebbles, sand, astroturf, etc., all cut into pieces

30cm (1 ft.) square
a blindfold

Let's take off our shoes and socks and turn on the sense of feeling in our toes and feet. This activity teaches the scientific concept of patterning in a fun way. It allows children to figure out, on their own, a sequence or pattern of textures which can be easily rearranged and changed to provide a variety of opportunities to develop the sense of touch. Touch with your toes as well as your fingers and experience the new sensations of touch under foot.

What to do

1. An adult, with a few children, constructs a texture road. The road should be constructed so that a specific pattern is repeated and developed with, at first, very contrasting textures. For example, soft (rug) / hard (wood),soft / hard, soft / hard, etc., or rough (doormat) / smooth (tile), rough / smooth, rough /smooth, etc. Later you can place more similar textures adjacent to each other to develop fine discrimination skills.

2. Blindfold one or two children at a time, take off their shoes and socks, and let them walk the texture road.

3. As the children walk, feeling the texture with their bare feet, each should pause and name or describe the texture. After naming the texture, they walk down the road to the next texture and name it. As they walk, the texture pattern is revealed.

4. After all the children have completed the course, change the road's texture pattern.

5. Proceed as above until all the children have taken a turn.

Want to do more?

Repeat above procedure using multi-textured objects, e.g., tile that is both hard and smooth. Have the children predict the next step of a predictable pattern. For example, if the pattern is hard, soft, hard, soft, etc. they could predict what the next step will bring.

SPACE HELMETS

Words you can use

helmet
space
astronaut
space shuttle
planets
stars
moon
gravity
launch

Things you will need

1 gallon plastic milk jugs

miscellaneous pieces of decorative material (for example, strips of colored transparent plastic from term paper covers, pipe cleaners, garbage bag ties, bread tags, bits of styrofoam)

white glue
razor blade or box cutter

permanent markers, scissors

The expanse of outer space holds many wonders for children of all ages. Hardly a day passes without seeing or hearing something related to space travel — real or imaginary. There are many concepts to be learned from outer space, yet in reality few of us will ever get there. Right? Wrong! We can get there in a few seconds if we are properly prepared. This activity gets the children into a proper frame of mind and prepares them for the delightful fantasy of journeying into space.

What to do

1. Using a razor blade or sharp scissors, cut the space helmet from the milk jug in the shape shown in the illustration. This should be done by an adult.

2. Decorate the helmet with objects from the materials suggested. Use white glue as needed. Younger children will probably need lots of help, but it will be worth it for the fun they'll have with the completed helmet. Cutting and decorating should be done in one session and the helmets set aside to dry thoroughly.

3. When the helmets are dry, the children can become space pioneers off to explore the far reaches of the galaxy.

Want to do more?

Space fantasies are fun to act out. Select a planet to visit or talk about travel to the moon. Build a space traveling machine from a large box. Allow each child a chance to visit another planet. Talk about the weightlessness and the absence of air to breathe. Talk about the differences between real space exploration, such as the space shuttle launches, and fantasy travel a la STAR WARS and E.T. Bring in books and magazines about space travel and outer space.

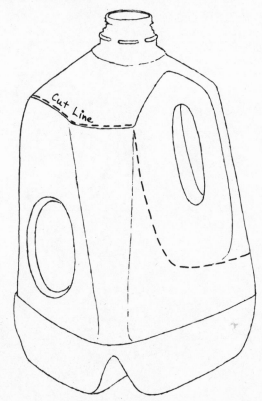

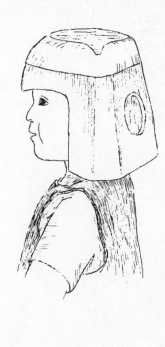

COLOR MAKERS

Words you can use

color names such as red, yellow, blue, etc.
match
partner
combine
closest
primary color
secondary color

Things you will need

pieces of colored acetate (ask local high school or college instructors to save their students term paper covers)

cut each cover in four pieces

music source — tape or record

Once children are able to identify colors by name, it's fun to begin learning about how colors combine to make new colors. COLOR MAKERS gives those who need it practice in combining primary colors to create secondary colors. Give a piece of the transparent plastic to each child and they become color makers!

What to do

1. Give each child a plastic "color maker". With most groups it would be wise to start with the primary colors — red, yellow, and blue. When the music starts, the children can dance and move around the room. When the music stops, they must stop and stand facing the person closest to them. In the beginning, some children will need help finding their partner. You may want to start and stop the music several times before playing the game to give the children some practice. Once they know what to do they'll be fine.

2. Start, then stop the music. When each child has a partner, have them put their color makers together. What color do they make? They may want to hold their squares up to the light for a better look. Say things like, "Yes, you two make green. Gina is yellow. Mark is blue. Yellow and blue make green. Did anybody else make green? Who made another color?

3. You may want to conclude the game by using a large piece of paper and crayons to write down some of the children's color combinations (see illustration) The color makers could also be hung in the windows in various arrangements to show the combinations the children have discovered.

Want to do more?

Make your own stained glass windows by cutting the plastic into shapes and taping them together. Bring in a real stained glass piece for the children to see. There may even be someone who would be willing to come in and demonstrate stained glass making for the children, as another experience of the beauty of light and color. See the index for several other color activities.

MARCHING OF THE SEASONS

Words you can use

march
season
seasonal names
listen
order
sequence

Things you will need

armbands or
headbands
displaying pictures
of the different
seasons

marching music

Children love to march. They can make their own music and move to it or they can listen to marching band records and strut around the room in time to the music. This marching activity teaches seasonal sequencing and lends itself to repetition for reinforcement of sequencing concepts.

What to do

1. Have the children line up in groups of four.

2. Distribute a different seasonal arm band to each of the four children in a group.

3. Before starting the music the teacher calls out "It's snowing!" At this cue the children in each group of four line up in the sequence of Winter, Spring, Summer, and Fall.

4. Start the music. The children begin to march around the room.

5. The music is stopped and the teacher calls out "The birds are building their nests!" At this cue, the children reorder their lines of four into the sequence of Spring, Summer, Fall, and Winter.

Then the music is resumed and the children may march.

6. The game continues with the teacher calling appropriate seasonal activities until each "season" has had a chance to lead the group.

7. This activity can be repeated, using different seasonal cues, as often as the interest of the children or the need for sequencing practice dictates.

Want to do more?

Sequence shades of a color, from dark to light or light to dark. Sequence pictures of people from infants to adults.

STEPPING OUT, HOP, SKIP, JUMP

Words you can use

words to describe
the moves you
choose

measure
compare
distance
faster
slower
longer
shorter
most
least
fewest

Things you will need

ruler
notebook
chalk
tape

Which is faster a hop, a skip, or a jump? Have a race to find out. Now look a little more closely at those movements. Some cover more distance than others. You can use this factor to create a measurement and counting experience. STEPPING OUT gives children a chance to practice hopping, skipping, and jumping, those very important gross motor skills, while exercising their thinking power in the process.

What to do

1. Use a piece of chalk or some tape to mark off a start and finish for STEPPING OUT. You will be counting the number of steps from point to point, so 2-3 meters (6-9 ft.) is just fine unless you have children who are very good at counting.

2. Choose a movement style that you wish to use such as a skip, a tip-toe, a regular step, a hop, or a jump.

3. Have the children measure the size of the step chosen by making chalk marks on the sidewalk. Obviously each child's step size will be different, but what we're looking for is a basis for comparing one type of movement to another.

4. Have a child travel from start to finish using the chosen step. Count the steps needed to travel this distance and write down the number. You may want to use simple drawings to illustrate the moves so that the children can "read" the results.

5. Choose another step and repeat the process. This time, however, stress a comparison of the length of the step and the resulting number of steps required. Experiment with a number of movements. Which require the least number of steps to travel from point to point? The most? Do the children begin to realize that the movements with the fewest number of steps are not necessarily the fastest ways to travel? Giant steps don't get you there as fast as running even if your feet don't touch the ground as many times. And, by the way, which moves are the most fun? Why not conclude with a free for all? Everyone choose a move and all step out together!

Want to do more?

Increase the distance between start and finish. Have the children predict which movement will require more or less steps. Use rulers to measure steps. Graph your results.

THE PURR-FECT SMELL

By having the children pretend to be cats as they cautiously creep up on the source of a scent, we can use fantasy play to find out about strength, diffusion, air currents and other factors which affect the sense of smell. THE PURR-FECT SMELL also provides an opportunity to work with measurement in a meaningful way. After working with a few smells, you and the children will realize that some spread very quickly, while others lose their scent. What else can your cats discover?

What to do

1. First, do a little warm-up without smells. Pretend to be kittens, moving and sniffing slowly and carefully around the room, to practice the technique.

2. Place a paper plate in the center of an open space. Indicate that a smell will be placed on that plate and that the children are to pretend they are cats creeping across the floor looking for the smell.

3. Have the children form a circle around the paper plate but at least six feet away.

4. Place the scent on the plate and have the children become cats searching for the smell. When a child first notices the smell, he or she should stop, roll over, and purr.

5. Mark the spot at which they first noticed the smell with a block. Measure the distance from the paper plate to each child's spot. Are they all about the same or are there some differences? Remember that the children may need practice learning to stop as soon as they smell the scent.

6. Open the door or turn on the fan. Disperse the odor and discuss the smell just experienced. Was the smell good? Strong? Bad? Use as many descriptive words as possible to identify the smell.

7. Try another scent. Try to determine which smell is stronger.

Want to do more?

Hide a scent in the classroom. See if the children can find and identify the odor. Try using one of the smells on a warm wash cloth. Does this make a difference? (It should, because odors are affected by temperature.) Are odors more easily detected in certain parts of the room? Why? Drafts, windows, doors, and competing odors are possible causes. Put popped popcorn in one corner of the room and have your "Cats" track the odor down. Set up an odor center with smell jars. How long does it takes before your noses can't smell an odor any more?

WEATHER PREDICTORS

Words you can use

weather
forecast
clouds
cirrus
cumulus
murky
dark
nimbus
hot
warm
cold
temperature
predict
stormy
rain
snow
sleet
weather report
wind
broadcast

Things you will need

laminated weather cards (teacher made) showing various weather conditions such as snow, rain, wind, hot weather, cold weather, (pictures can be of children and adults in various weather conditions)

a toy microphone or remote microphone

a song about weather

What's the weather going to be? This is a question that children hear almost everyday of their lives as they observe their parents listening to the weather forecast on the radio and television. Can children make forecasts? We think so! In the process, they learn about observation and prediction as well as weather and the signs it gives forecasters for their broadcasts.

What to do

1. Gather the children around at circle time. Sing a song about the weather. Pass the weather picture cards out face down so that each child has one. Ask the children what the weather is like today. Is it hot? Is it cold? Is it snowing? Is it windy?

2. After the children have described the current conditions have them turn over their cards. The child or children who have cards that match the day's current weather stand and come to the center of the circle. These children are then given a toy microphone and are asked to give the weather forecast for the afternoon or for the next day using their pictures as cues to give their best "guesstimates" as to what the coming weather will be.

3. The children who are not forecasters can prepare a daily weather calendar based upon the forecasters' predictions. They can discuss the accuracy or inaccuracy of the forecasts each day. Class discussion can also focus around what weather forecasters use for their predictions such as cloud formations, temperature, and wind.

Want to do more?

Keep a chart for a month showing simple daily weather symbols. Let the children count the days it rained, snowed, etc. for a total month. Bar graphs of weather conditions can be made and compared. Watch or listen to some real weather reports on radio or television. How can you make yours more realistic? THE CLOUD BOOK by Tomie de Paola has simple and accurate descriptions of cloud formations along with the correct names.

FLASHLIGHT TAG

Words you can use

beam
light
intensity
straight line
flashlight
dark

Things you will need

a flashlight (4 celled)that casts a long, narrow beam of light

a darkened room with furniture or boxes to hide behind

a record player with appropriate music (i.e., slow if you want the children to move slowly, or fast if they will be moving quickly from one hiding place to another)

Lights flashing on the wall, tracing paths of light across the ceiling with a flashlight, or playing catch with spots of light on the floor — all these activities focus the attention of any child on light. With that focus, this variation of flashlight tag teaches, through play, some of the simple characteristics of light.

What to do

1. The room is darkened and the teacher holds the flashlight.

2. When the music starts, the children may move about the room. They may need to be reminded not to run.

3. When the music stops, they must stop. Then shine the light around the room. Anyone touched by the light must stand up. (They may still play but cannot bend over or crouch behind things to hide.)

4. Play ceases when all are standing.

5. After the game has been played several times, discuss what the children know about light. The ideas you may have discovered are: light travels in a straight line, and light cannot travel through things.

Want to do more?

Have one teacher hold a mirror—reflected light will catch children behind things. Using one flashlight and a number of mirrors, set up a sequence of reflections to form a light maze. Use different colored filters over the flashlight.

THE SHAPE AND HOP GAME

Words you can use

shape words
match
cooperate
team
partner
pair

Things you will need

a large piece of plastic, such as a window shade

a permanent marking pen

2 sets of cards with shapes drawn on them — solid shapes rather than outlines.

The shape and hop game promotes active cooperation between children as they work together to identify shapes while moving along a game path. They have to think together and move together, a real challenge. What is especially nice is that a child who knows the shapes can be teamed with a less skilled child so that both benefit not only from peer teaching, but from the cooperation that is involved in the hopping, thinking, and playing of the game.

What to do

1. Prepare a game trail on the large piece of plastic using the marker. The trail should be wide enough to accommodate 2 children side by side. Decorate the open space on one side of the trail. Make it as interesting as you like. Be creative.

2. Prepare 2 sets of shape cards. If possible, laminate these or cover them with clear contact paper. One set will be placed randomly, face down, on the spaces of the plastic playing sheet. The other set will be displayed next to the playing sheet.

3. Use the cards to review the shapes before beginning the game.

4. Game Rules:

　　1. The game is played with partners. Each team must jump together from one square to another while holding hands. The "togetherness" can be as precise or as flexible as you wish, depending on the skills of the children.

2. When the team enters a square with a card, one of the partners reaches down and picks up the shape card. The card is shown to the other partner who looks at the displayed set of shape cards to find the matching shape.

3. The matching card is brought back to the game sheet and confirmed.

4. The team hops to the next card and repeats the matching activity. The children should take turns picking up and matching the cards as the game proceeds.

5. They move through the game board until all the cards have been matched. If during the game any match is incorrect, the child is to return to the display set to try again.

6. Separate the pairs of the cards, shuffle, and reset the game board. Hop another game.

Want to do more?

Change the match to number or letter match, color match, or any other skill that needs practice. Add "Go Back" cards or "Advance" cards. Combine skills in a color and shape, or color, shape, and size match.

HODGE PODGE

TORNADO IN A JAR

Making a tornado jar is simple. However, holding the jar just right so that the water swirls to form the tornado requires practice and is not easy to do. It's a fun item for the science table and the persistent child will soon learn to use it. Once one child has acquired the technique, others will soon follow. Note: Tornado air movement is in a clockwise direction. Be sure to spin your jar in that direction if you want to replicate a "real" tornado.

Things you will need

tall clear plastic jar

4 to 6 small balls of aluminum foil

clear liquid soap
water
blue food coloring

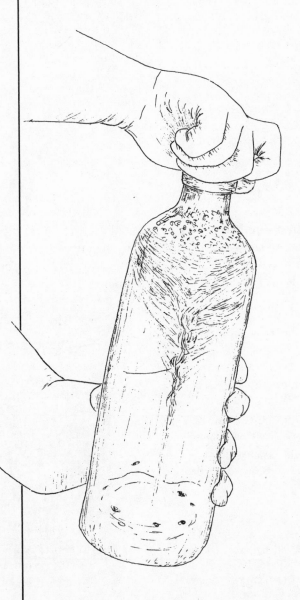

What to do

1. Place a teaspoon (5 ml) of clear liquid soap in your plastic container.

2. Drop into the jar 3-4 very small pieces of aluminum foil rolled into balls. The foil should be folded and pressed so that it will sink.

3. Fill the jar to the top with water.

4. Add 1-2 drops of blue food coloring.

5. Rotate the container and a swirling effect should be produced. It may take some practice. Set the container up on the table and watch. The force of the foil at the bottom should keep the water in motion. This action resembles the motion set up as circular rotations of air in the atmosphere form a tornado.

OCEAN IN A JAR

Things you will need

blue food coloring

clear turpentine (available at drugstores)

water

a tall clear plastic container with a leak proof lid, such as a dish soap bottle

Ocean in a jar is a great plaything to have on the science table. Children can create it themselves with minimal adult assistance and it's something nearly everyone enjoys handling.

What to do

1. Fill a clear container 1/2 full of water.

2. Add one to two drops of blue food coloring.

3. Fill to the top with clear turpentine, and seal.

4. Place in the hands of the children. Tell them to hold it sideways.

5. With just a gentle shake, wave after wave will fill their ocean in a jar.

CRITTER CAGE

Things you will need

two tops from five gallon plastic paint containers

hardware cloth (wire) from the hardware store

wire cutters
sawdust
paper
water
food for the critter

You may want to build simple cages for occasional visiting critters. An aquarium is a fine container for keeping animals, but occasionally you may want a lighter, more portable "critter cage" for field trips or outside. This cage can be made from easily obtainable items and is fairly easy to construct and later store.

What to do

1. Cut out a piece of hardware cloth (wire) the diameter of your lids plus a few centimeters, and as long as you want the cage to be.

2. Roll the wire into one of the lids. It should fit with a few centimeters overlap. (see drawing)

3. Place the second lid on top of the wire. Your cage is now built. If you want to be fancy, cut a door.

4. This cage is good for small mammals, frogs, lizards, butterflies, or large insects. Snakes are best kept in a glass aquarium where they won't cut themselves.

5. Supply your critter with water, food, grass, leaves, or whatever seems necessary. Keep it no longer than a week. Study it and then release it. No wild animal deserves to spend its life in a cage. If an insect lays eggs, be sure to take them outside, too, or you'll have little tiny babies everywhere.

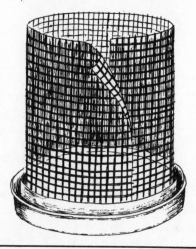

HANGER SORTER

Simple cards and objects easily hang on the paper clip hooks of the Hanger Sorter to provide a quiet activity that develops sequencing skills. It's another way to make a "ho hum" activity a little more lively.

wire clothes hangers
string
paperclips

objects that are related to each other in a sequence (Those that cannot be hung should be placed on a card that has had a hole punched in the top.)

What to do?

1. Prepare the coat hanger sorter by tying 5 or 6 pieces of string along the bar of the hanger. Glue the strings in place with white glue so that they are spaced evenly along the entire length of the coat hanger. Allow the glue to dry, then tie a paperclip hook to the end of each string.

2. Prepare sequencing items by sorting sets of items into separate containers.
   - A. Set of buttons from large to small
   - B. Set of buttons from light to dark
   - C. Life cycle of a frog or insect on cards
   - D. History of a family sequence cards
     i.e., Greatgrandpa, Grandpa, Dad, Me
   - E. Rainbow color sequence on cards
   - F. Number sequence on card, e.g. 51, 52, 53, 54, 55, 56

3. Demonstrate how to use the hanger sorter, then keep it in an accessible place such as on the edge of a table, or on a hook near the science table.

4. Have the children place the objects in sequence on the hooks.

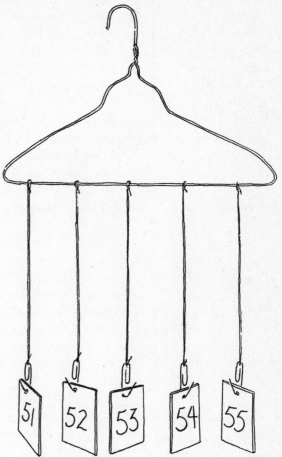

Gryphon House, Inc.
Box 275
Mt. Rainier MD 20712
   Hug A Tree And Other Things To Do Outdoors With Young Children by Rockwell, Sherwood and Williams (the authors of this book). Write for a free catalog.

National Science Teacher Association
1742 Connecticut Avenue N.W.
Washington DC 20009
   Science And Children — journal
   Early Childhood And Science — book
   Write for list of publications.

The Young Naturalist Foundation
c/o Owl Chickadee Magazines
255 Great Arrow Avenue
Buffalo NY 14027
   Owl magazine — elementary children
   Chickadee magazine — preschool children
   Dr. Zed's Dazzling Book of Science Activities
   Write for list of publications.

National Aeronautics and Space Administration
Washington DC 20546
   A variety of resources including speakers, films and teaching ideas.

National Audubon Society
950 Third Avenue
New York NY 10022
   Teacher resources.

National Geographic Society
17th and M Streets NW
Washington DC 20036
   National Geographic World magazine —
   elementary children
   Teacher resources.

INDEX

absorb 77, 81, 94, 97, 125
activity chart 22
adult roles 7, 8, 14, 18, 23, 30, 43, 55, 94, 104, 115, 117, 126, 131, 134, 141-143, 152
air 18, 29, 31, 52, 64, 65, 78, 92, 93, 104, 143, 147, 151
anatomy 32, 107, 114, 117, 118, 140
animals 74, 117, 134, 136, 140, 152
area 49, 93, 103
art activities (see PAINTS AND PRINTS, page 77)
astronomy 37, 143

balance 17, 47, 50, 65, 95
basic food groups 108, 119
birds 34, 123, 136, 145
bones 21, 44, 107, 117
bubbles 29, 92, 96

calendar 67, 111, 148
cause and effect 20, 50, 65, 92
change 18, 20, 48, 51, 53, 54, 56, 66, 77-79, 84, 129
chart 22, 37, 70, 82, 101, 119, 123, 148
chemistry 92, 99, 100
child development 20
child-directed learning 20, 21
circle time 13, 21, 36, 47, 57, 59, 82, 100, 107, 109, 112, 127, 140, 142, 145, 148, 152, 153
classification 27, 39, 49, 64, 68, 86, 110, 116, 131, 140
clouds 12, 64, 66, 67, 91, 104, 148
collecting 15, 17, 20, 27, 28, 39-41, 43, 49, 51, 53, 56, 64, 70, 78, 80, 92, 95, 97, 102, 123, 124, 126, 128, 129, 130, 134-136, 139
colors 18, 61, 69, 78-81, 83, 87, 91, 94, 96, 108, 125, 128-130, 144
communication 33, 36, 44
concept map 21, 24
construction 37, 45, 50, 56, 69, 84, 88, 93, 117
counting 33, 40, 49, 55, 65, 69, 70, 123, 127-130, 146, 148

creative movement 47, 61, 107, 117, 139
curriculum planning 8
cycles 12, 21, 28, 67, 104, 153

dinosaurs 55, 57, 71, 140
dramatic play 34, 50, 67, 68, 74, 143

electricity 18, 38, 64, 65
energy 18, 53, 62, 66, 73
equipment & materials 13-16, 21, 27-31, 34, 41, 48, 52, 53, 101, 154
estimate 129, 133
evaluation 8
evaporation 11, 21, 56, 91, 93, 97, 101, 104, 135
experiment 23, 31, 44, 47, 48, 51, 53, 61, 64, 70, 72, 77, 78, 83, 91, 93, 97-102, 108, 135, 146
eye droppers 78, 94

fall (Autumn) 28, 68, 80, 83, 124, 127, 129, 130, 145
field trips and walks (see OUTDOOR SCIENCE, page 121) 27, 28, 39, 41, 42, 50, 52, 54, 83, 77, 88, 95, 102, 110, 152
fine motor skills 41, 47, 49, 55
fish 32, 95, 134
following directions 94, 107, 118
food experiences (see HEALTH & NUTRITION, page 105), 100
friction 18, 51, 88
funnel 98, 102

games 24, 27, 35, 36, 40, 49, 74, 84, 107, 116, 118, 119, 141, 144, 145, 149, 150
graphing 69, 119
gross motor development 68, 146
growth 7, 18, 20, 42, 112, 115, 127, 139

habitat 28
Halloween 21, 107
holidays 77, 80

identification 27, 134
inclined plane 51, 53
independent activities 24, 47, 48-53, 126, 152-154
insects 27, 28, 123, 128, 131, 134, 152
integrated approach 8

juice 67, 92, 103, 108, 120, 123

language development
  expressive 11, 12, 32, 33, 34, 36, 39, 43, 52, 54, 71, 100, 110, 136, 126, 128, 131, 142, 147
  written 13, 51, 53, 67, 70, 128
  vocabulary 11, 12, 34, 36, 43, 55, 66, 96
leaves 27, 28, 36, 77, 80, 83, 84, 123, 124, 127, 128-131, 141, 152
lesson plans 23
light 34, 37, 64, 65, 104, 112, 125
listening 35, 44, 63-65, 100, 109, 114, 136, 145, 148
lotto 27, 141

machines, simple 48, 51, 53
magnets 8, 18, 24, 30, 70, 87
magnify 126, 84
mastery learning 19
matching 35-37, 39, 47, 49, 69, 74, 84, 85, 101, 103, 107, 110, 128, 140, 141, 144, 148, 150
matter, phases of 31, 66
measurement 45, 49, 79, 98, 101, 131
memory 11, 35, 40, 41, 74, 136
moon 7, 18, 67, 143
mud 56
museum 27, 70

night 37, 67, 73, 119, 120, 130
nutrition 105

observations 23, 27, 28, 32, 33, 42, 52, 57, 61, 62, 65, 67, 77, 79, 86, 91-93, 95, 96, 99, 102, 104, 108, 109, 111, 123, 127, 133, 134, 148
ocean 13, 32, 152
occupations 37, 39, 41, 50, 52, 56, 64, 77, 83, 114, 120, 135, 144, 148

parents 13, 15-17, 37, 67, 108, 111, 115, 119, 148
photosynthesis 139
physics 31, 44, 48, 51-53
planning 7, 8, 20, 21, 23
plants 18, 33, 42, 71, 77, 94, 102, 128, 139
prediction 42, 51, 53, 67, 95, 100, 120, 148
problem solving 12, 20, 49, 51, 95, 103, 126
puzzles 24, 41, 49, 52, 92

questions with children 8, 9, 32

rain 12, 17, 66, 68, 79, 82, 88, 104, 133, 135, 139, 148
readiness skills 13, 27, 34, 35, 36, 40, 43, 49, 63, 64, 69, 70, 86, 94, 107, 118, 128, 131, 136, 142, 144, 150
recording data 42, 53, 61, 64, 69, 70, 82, 119, 131, 133, 134, 135, 136, 144, 149
resources 11, 15, 56, 67, 154
rocks 27, 39, 42, 54, 70, 98, 100

safety 14, 65, 86
scavenger hunt 131
science kits 24
science organizations 15
science storage 13
seasons 21, 27, 68, 82, 101, 104, 131, 134, 135, 145, 148
seeds 33, 42, 72, 102, 139
self-awareness 11, 12, 18-19, 86, 107, 111, 114, 115, 118, 140
senses 18, 35, 36, 41, 43, 44, 52, 63, 64, 88, 101, 114, 124, 131, 136, 142, 147
sequence 7, 20, 40, 142, 145, 149, 153
shadows 34, 74, 84
shapes 29, 34, 36, 37, 49, 50, 61, 67, 69, 74, 86, 139, 144, 150
shells 24, 27, 36, 40, 71, 85
sight 35, 36, 74
sink and float 31, 61, 92, 95, 151
skeleton 28, 107, 117
smelling 35, 92, 108, 110, 147
snow 56, 66, 68, 82, 91, 125, 148
soil 17, 18, 28, 42, 56, 102, 139
sorting 27, 44, 71, 80, 85
sound 18, 35, 44, 52, 63-65, 82, 109, 114, 134, 136
space 7, 12, 18, 29, 31, 40, 51, 67, 78, 84, 143, 147, 150
spring (mechanical) 41

spring (season) 68, 93, 127, 145

stars 18, 37, 67, 143

stethoscope 114

summer 21, 68, 77, 94, 145

sun 18, 56, 68, 73, 84, 104, 125, 129, 139

tape recorder 64, 136

taste 35, 100, 108, 110, 112, 113

teeth 27, 57, 64, 118, 120

temperature 54, 66, 68, 96, 101, 112, 113, 125, 147, 148

texture 27, 33, 35, 39, 43, 108, 110, 124, 131, 142

thermometer 17, 66, 68, 101, 125

time 8, 11, 12, 54, 65, 67, 93, 97, 111, 141

touch 20, 33, 35-38, 43, 87, 107, 118, 140, 142, 146

toys 47, 51, 62, 97

tweezers 41, 126

unit topics 21

   animals 18, 32, 34, 37, 54, 57, 71, 114, 116, 117, 134, 140, 152

   colors 18, 61, 69, 78-81, 83, 87, 91, 94, 96, 108, 125, 128-130, 144

   dinosaurs 24, 55, 57, 71, 140

   energy 18, 53, 62, 66, 73

   farming 21

   Halloween 21, 107

   insects 27, 126, 134, 152

   magnets 1, 3, 8, 14, 17, 19, 21, 24, 25, 30, 45, 57, 70, 75, 87, 89, 105, 121, 137, 151

   ocean 13, 152

   plants 18, 21, 32, 42, 71, 80, 108, 110, 134, 139

   rocks 17, 18, 24, 27, 28, 32, 36, 39, 40, 42, 43, 55, 62, 95

   seasons 21, 27, 68, 82, 101, 104, 131, 134, 135, 145, 148

   seeds 17, 19, 27, 33, 40, 42, 72, 77, 112, 139

   self-awareness 11, 12, 18-19, 86, 107, 111, 114, 115, 118, 140

   senses 23, 24, 35, 110

   simple machines 48, 51, 53

   sink and float 31, 61, 92, 95, 151

   transportation 21, 77

   trees 39, 127, 129, 130, 139

   weather 21, 38, 54, 68, 82, 91, 101, 104, 123, 127, 135, 148

visual memory 11, 41

water 11, 12, 18, 21, 24, 31, 32, 37, 39, 42, 54, 56, 61, 63, 64, 66, 72, 77-79, 81, 83, 84, 91-97, 99-104, 109, 112, 117, 120, 125, 127, 133, 135, 139, 151, 152

weight 29, 47, 57, 71, 93, 95, 115

wind 11, 18, 29, 42, 82, 84, 88, 148

winter 28, 37, 54, 67, 68, 88, 110, 128, 129, 145

zero 70

The Instant Curriculum:
500 Developmentally Appropriate Learning Activities for Busy Teachers of Young Children

Pam Schiller and Joan Rossano

This is a practical book. 500 learning activities are ready to use with a minimum of planning and preparation. They are educationally sound and developmentally appropriate. These simple, effective activities will keep children's attention and interest every day.

A busy teacher will find this collection indispensable. A quick look through *The Instant Curriculum* will provide an endless supply of activities and projects. Many require no advance preparation at all. The book is profusely illustrated, clearly showing what to do and how to do it. The activities are conveniently grouped in curriculum areas. A month-by-month activity guide along with a thorough index help to locate exactly the right activity for nearly any purpose.

ISBN 0-87659-124-1

Story S-t-r-e-t-c-h-e-r-s:
Activities to Expand Children's Favorite Books

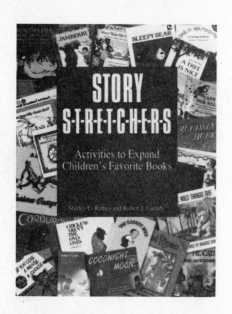

Shirley C. Raines and Robert J. Canady

Children love to hear and look at good books. Here is a perfect way to connect children's enthusiasm for books with other areas of the curriculum. *Story S-t-r-e-t-c-h-e-r-s* are teaching plans based on the stories in outstanding picture books that are among children's favorites.

Here are 450 teaching ideas to expand the interest of 90 different books. These ideas are organized around eighteen units commonly taught in the early childhood classroom.

"*Story S-t-r-e-t-c-h-e-r-s* is the best thing to happen to story time in decades. It should be the bible of every preschool and early primary teacher in America. Even better, it can be used just as easily by parents. Nothing I've seen approaches it in practicality and originality."—Jim Trelease, Author *The New Read Aloud Handbook*

ISBN 0-87659-119-5

The Learning Circle:
A Preschool Teacher's Guide to Circle Time

Patty Claycomb

Hundreds of circle time activities make this a necessary book. Activities can be used again and again because they give children a chance to talk about themselves and their friends. There are learning circle activities for every month, day, and season. Patty Claycomb knows how to weave a spirit of magic and adventure into the daily classroom.

ISBN 0-87659-115-2

Hug a Tree and Other Things to
Do Outdoors With Young Children

*Robert E. Rockwell, Elizabeth A. Sherwood, and
Robert A. Williams*

Hug a Tree experiences will help children ages three to seven learn to love and appreciate the natural environment anywhere. Each learning experience has a suggested age level, a clear description of what will be done, and suggestions for follow-up learning. Activities come under the headings of *Loving Your Environment, Turning On Your Senses, Backyard Data Collecting, Want to Know How Much?* and *Watching Time and Seasons.*

ISBN 0-87659-105-5

More Mudpies to Magnets:
Science for Young Children

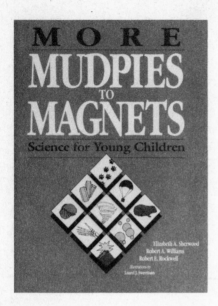

Elizabeth A. Sherwood, Robert A. Williams, Robert E. Rockwell

Here are 200 more pages of ready-to-use science experiments. The science skills developed by the activities in this book include classification, measuring, using space and time relationships, communication, predicting and inferring, and numbers. The chapters include:

- Chapter 1—Colors, Crystals, and Creations: Chemistry Beginnings
- Chapter 2—How Things Work: First Physics
- Chapter 3—Digging in the Dirt: Earth Explorations
- Chapter 4—How Hot, How Cold, How Windy, How Wet: Weather Watchers
- Chapter 5—Aerial Acrobatics: Flight and Space
- Chapter 6—Roots and Shoots: All About Plants
- Chapter 7—Houses for Snugs, Hideouts for Hamsters: Animal Adventures
- Chapter 8—Hodge Podge

ISBN 0-87659-150-0

Do Touch: Instant, Easy, Hands-On
Learning Experiences for Young Children

LaBritta Gilbert

This unique book of hands-on activities is designed to surround children with things to explore, wonder about, do and discover. These activities can be prepared quickly and easily from simple materials such as cups, sponges, craft sticks, corks, rice, and sandpaper. The chapters focus on pairing and puzzling, forming, fitting, categorizing, measuring and sorting and more. Clear directions and objectives are aided by expert illustrations.

ISBN 0-87659-118-7